ANARCHISM

Twayne's Studies in
Intellectual and Cultural History

Michael Roth, General Editor
Scripps College and the Claremont Graduate School

ANARCHISM

Richard D. Sonn

Twayne Publishers • New York
Maxwell Macmillan Canada • Toronto
Maxwell Macmillan International • New York Oxford Singapore Sydney

Anarchism

Twayne's Studies in Intellectual and Cultural History Series, No. 4

Twayne Publishers   Maxwell Macmillan Canada, Inc.
Macmillan Publishing Company   1200 Eglinton Avenue East
866 Third Avenue   Suite 200
New York, New York 10022   Don Mills, Ontario M3C 3N1

Macmillan Publishing Company is part of the Maxwell Communication
Group of Companies.

The paper used in this publication meets the minimum requirements
of American National Standard for Information Sciences—Permanence
of Paper for Printed Library Materials. ANSI Z3948-1984.∞™

10 9 8 7 6 5 4 3 2 1 (hc)

10 9 8 7 6 5 4 3 2 1 (pb)

Printed and bound in the United States of America.

Library of Congress Cataloging-in-Publication Data

Sonn, Richard David.
    Anarchism / Richard D. Sonn.
        p. cm. — (Twayne's studies in intellectual and cultural
    history ; no. 4)
    Includes bibliographical references and index.
    ISBN 0-8057-8611-2 (cl). — ISBN 0-8057-8636-8 (pb)
    1. Anarchism—History I. Title. II. Series.
HX828.S636 1992
335'.83—dc20   92-16954
                                          CIP

Contents

Acknowledgments

This book was written during the summer and fall of 1991, at a time of momentous change in the Soviet Union that could not fail to affect a history of European leftist thought. I am grateful to the Fulbright College of Arts and Sciences for granting me a leave that autumn to pursue this project. My colleagues in the department of history, Evan Bukey and Robert Finlay, were kind enough to read first drafts of my manuscript. I appreciate the help and support of the general editor of this series, Michael Roth, for his critical reading, and to my editor at Twayne, Jacob Conrad, for bringing the book to press so promptly. I would also like to record my indebtedness to Paul Avrich, dean of anarchist historians, whose many books portray incisively the variety of remarkable individuals who created the anarchist movement. All of the above individuals have improved this book; its faults are my own.

Thanks are due also to Mary Kirkpatrick for her help in preparing the manuscript. I appreciate the fortitude and forbearance shown by my wife Mary over the years. I would like to dedicate this book to my brother Don, who has made me appreciate the value of freedom, all too often taken for granted.

Fayetteville, Arkansas
July, 1992

Foreword

Twayne's Studies in Intellectual and Cultural History consists of brief original studies of major movements in European intellectual and cultural history, emphasizing historical approaches to continuity and change in religion, philosophy, political theory, aesthetics, literature, and science. The series reflects the recent resurgence of innovative contextual as well as theoretical work in these areas, and the more general interest in the study of ideas and cultures. It will advance some of the most exciting work in the human sciences as it stimulates further interest in cultural and intellectual history. The books are intended for the educated reader and the serious student; each combines the virtues of accessibility with original interpretations of important topics.

Richard Sonn's book surveys anarchism throughout the nineteenth and twentieth centuries in Europe and the United States. The study provides a rich portrait of anarchism as a political movement, concentrating particularly on the problems and possibilities of anarchist political theory. Sonn discusses the specific forms that anarchism has taken as a radical political movement in diverse national and cultural contexts. He emphasizes the anarchist drive for freedom from authoritarianism, and the alternative the movement posed to Marxism over the last century and a half. The book offers a fine balance between synthesis and analysis, and weaves together cultural, intellectual, and political history. Anarchism emerges as a body of ideas, but also as a way of life and as a commitment to a vision of utopia. The reader comes to understand the diversity of anarchisms, and the attempts to live out some of its ideas. Sonn emphasizes that with the demise of Marxism, this commitment and vision may yet become important again.

Richard Sonn's history of anarchism is an exploration of what made anarchism compelling to diverse groups of people in a variety of historical settings. He shows how the commitment to a radical conception of freedom inspired historical actors and thinkers throughout the industrializing world. This conception of freedom and the praxis that went along with it took several forms in a variety of historical contexts. Sonn's study provides the tools for understanding the theory and the political engagement that make anarchism an important part of the history of our present.

Michael S. Roth
Scripps College and the
Claremont Graduate School

Preface

Imagine a student who, having heard an inspiring lecture on anarchism, is interested in learning more about it. He or she consults a standard Western civilization text, perhaps, and finds very little: probably some mention of the Russian anarchist Mikhail Bakunin, presented as the foe of Karl Marx; perhaps a brief mention of anarchist terrorism in the 1890s or anarchist involvement in the Spanish civil war. Not satisfied with these snippets, the resolute student decides to try the college library, and finds him or herself wandering among the stacks marked "HX." After walking through perhaps an entire aisle of books devoted to the ideas of Marx and to socialism and communism, the student comes upon a section concerning communes. Next comes utopian communities, then the "utopian socialists" scornfully relegated to cloud-cuckoo-land by Marx, and then some intriguing books on utopian thought. Beyond utopia lies anarchism.

Unless the student ponders this search process, he or she may not consider the implications of the historiographical and spatial treatment of anarchism just encountered. Anarchism has been effectively dismissed as marginal, as a footnote to the really important revolutionary movement called Marxism. Why? Because Marxists can claim some impressive successes, while anarchists are stigmatized as failures. The key reason for their failure is suggested by their placement on the shelves. Anarchists were, at best, hopeless dreamers, unless their despair drove them to commit acts of terror, in which case they become the sinister figures of literary legend, lurking near Greenwich Observatory or some crowded café clutching a primitive bomb. The bombers have passed from idealism to nihilism; in either case their revolt against society has been judged ineffectual. Compared to the massed blue-clad marchers filing by in disciplined order on May Day or some other Socialist holiday, the anarchist appears as a lone wolf, irrelevant indeed.

The historian of anarchism must therefore be a debunker of stereotypes. He must reclaim for anarchism the place it deserves among the political and social ideologies that have arisen since the French Revolution. Along with liberalism, conservatism, and socialism, anarchism emerged in direct response to the vast social changes affecting Europe in the nineteenth century. The ideas of an impressive series of anarchist thinkers had found favor with millions of followers by the late nineteenth century. In assessing the major contributions to nineteenth-century political thought, the history textbook of a century ago would likely have included the writings of Pierre-Joseph Proudhon, Mikhail Bakunin, and Peter Kropotkin alongside those of Edmund Burke, John Stuart Mill, Alexis de Tocqueville, and Karl Marx. In the last third of the nineteenth century, anarchism vied with socialism for the allegiance of the working classes and attracted a considerable number of sympathizers among the more privileged classes. It was not until the joint cataclysms of the First World War and the Russian Revolution that anarchism appeared to be definitively superseded by Marxism. After 1918, anarchism rapidly succumbed to the onslaught of international socialism on the one hand, and to Fascist hypernationalism on the other. At a time when the power of the state grew to be so enormous that a new term, *totalitarianism,* was needed to describe its all-embracing power, what else could a movement such as anarchism, dedicated to the abolition of the state, seem to be except irrelevant? Two world wars, the tremendous growth in the democracies of big government and the welfare state, the huge scale of government and corporate bureaucracies—all seemed to justify consigning anarchism to never-never land.

Our inquiring student, browsing in the obscure anarchist corner of the stacks, would soon find that twentieth-century histories of anarchism have lost the shrill and alarmist tone of turn-of-the-century accounts and have usually adopted the elegiac tone used to describe the history of a failure. While conceding the irrelevance of the movement, they recognize that anarchism was an authentic response to the dual revolution of the nineteenth century, the capitalist-industrial and the liberal-democratic, and so deserves its proper if limited place. If the student happens to encounter a Marxist analysis of anarchism, he or she will probably be convinced that anarchism was a quaintly primitive, instinctual revolt of prepolitical groups such as peasants and handworkers, groups that had themselves been consigned to the "dustbin of history" by the march of modernity. In short, the student will probably be confirmed in his or her sense of anarchism's marginality.

But anarchism was more than a political theory of freedom from domination by any and all authority; it was a faith, and a way of life, that exercised a powerful hold over the imagination. People did not simply understand anarchist ideas; they lived them. There has always been an existential element to anarchism that transcends dogma. The astute reader will not simply understand the ideas contained in anarchism, but will also be able to analyze the modern world from an anarchist perspective so as to grasp the core of why anarchism attracted so many.

It is my contention that anarchism should not be treated nostalgically. If it can no longer claim to represent a mass movement, it remains a valid critical tool. It may even be premature to write off anarchism as a viable political movement. In our own rapidly changing world at the end of the twentieth century, with communism increasingly being spoken of in the past tense and while that other triumphant modern ideology, nationalism, is being assailed by long-submerged regional identities on the one hand and international associations on the other, it seems appropriate to look anew at anarchist analyses. History is an interplay between the present and the past; a history of anarchism written in the 1990s must necessarily differ from those written at midcentury when the nation-state seemed triumphant and communism still a movement of the future.

In Chapter 1 of this book, I would like to continue using the spatial metaphor of the library shelves to describe anarchism's place in the political spectrum of nineteenth-century Europe, and to locate the sources of its appeal in geographic and social terms. Rather than treating the anarchist movement in isolation, anarchist ideas and their popular appeal will be contrasted with those of other radical and leftist groups. The fundamental question posed by historians— Why *then*?—brings us to the temporal realm, to anarchism's midnineteenth-century genesis as a coherent (but always evolving) ideology. People have long dreamed of a realm of total freedom, yet despite precursors as varied as Lao-tze and Diderot, anarchism as an historical movement could not have emerged before the nineteenth century, nor outside of Europe. The anarchists were both inspired and troubled by the series of political revolutions that rocked Europe after 1789, and they developed their own critique of the failure of these revolutions that differed markedly from those of contemporary socialists and conservatives. Even the anarchist sense of time—simultaneously nostalgic, apocalyptic, and utopian—differed from liberal and socialist notions of temporality.

Of all the new ideologies that emerged in the nineteenth century, anarchism maintained the greatest fidelity to the Enlightenment's distinction between natural and civil law, retaining a primarily moral vision of a purer and simpler society that would not swamp the individual with the mass. The anarchists believed in a natural society that would not submit human reason or sensuality to religious repression. This notion of the free, expressive individual was modern, not traditional, and it emerged in the eighteenth century with the breakup of the older, corporate society. Nevertheless anarchist thinkers hearkened back to the corporate order of medieval society, though not to feudal hierarchy (they were selectively nostalgic). Anarchists would always be torn between the conflicting attractions of individual freedom and social solidarity, the worlds of the Enlightenment and the medieval commune.

In subsequent chapters I will trace the heritage of anarchist thought, placing it in the context of the evolving anarchist understanding of how to create an extrapolitical order that might guarantee freedom without domination. From this intellectual vantage point, we will descend to the anarchist movement itself and explore its evolution through the First World War and into the Russian Revolution, when anarchists briefly vied with the Bolsheviks for control. And in the last two chapters I will consider the impact of anarchism on the twentieth century. Chapter 4 will focus on Spanish anarchism, culminating in the Spanish civil war, when anarchists came as close as they ever have to seizing power and turning their ideas into reality. Finally, in Chapter 5, we will look at the contemporary scene, exploring anarchistic trends as demonstrated in the youth counterculture of the 1960s, the radical ecology movement and the rise of Green parties, the anarchist philosophy of Murray Bookchin, the novels of Edward Abbey, and other signs of continuing anarchist vitality.

With the rapid decline, perhaps even demise, of Marxism and its claim to represent the future of history, and with the seeming triumph of liberal capitalism and its vast consumer culture, it is all the more important to recapture the censure of domination and alienation central to the profoundly misunderstood movement known as anarchism. Not only were anarchist thinkers of a century ago often more accurate than socialists in judging the revolutionary potential of the oppressed, they also better foresaw the human and political implications of a revolutionary seizure of power and its institutionalization in a one-party state. It is instructive to consider why anarchists have largely failed to achieve their goals.

1

The Place of Anarchism

Let us take another glance at our generic Western civilization text, this time to note how difficult it is to present the course of European history in other than progressive terms. Leaving aside the ancient world and looking back only to the last millennium, our inquiring student sees the emergence of feudalism from the chaos of the Dark Ages. The high Middle Ages saw glorious Gothic cathedrals built while knights idealized themselves in chivalric terms. Towns arose, obtaining charters from kings to guarantee their liberty from local lords, and society became more complex as it grew away from the decentralized and rural life known by most medieval peasants. Then came the dynamic era of the Renaissance and the Reformation, and the illiterate, tradition-bound medieval peasant became a questing individual. New monarchs grasped for institutional rather than merely personal power; royal bureaucracies helped buttress their control of once-powerful nobles and keep the tax revenues flowing in. All subsequent developments served to increase centralized royal control. Even the French Revolution—while toppling a king—consolidated power in the state, with Napoleon as the immediate beneficiary.

Simultaneously with the democratic revolutions of the late eighteenth century came the industrial revolution, offering vastly increased power both to the entrepreneurs who developed the new machines and the factory system of work and to the states who harnessed its power. In terms of accumulated knowledge, wealth, and power, the midnineteenth century looked down from a dizzying height on the ignorant peasants and craftsmen of the past, and not just from a sense of material improvement. Citizens felt themselves vastly more free than their downtrodden ancestors, due to revolutions and to the Enlightenment's concept of human rights that even kings dared not transgress. Freedom was exemplified in new constitutions; wealth, in cities and factories; and both were guaranteed by the order of centralized states. This progressive narrative has been complicated by the incursion of social history into the story of power, so our student's Western civilization text will dutifully include aspects of the everyday life of the masses. For histories written from the midnineteenth to the midtwentieth century, the rise of nationalism was *the* story.

From the anarchists' point of view, that story was a disaster. All the dominant forces of the modern world guaranteed the average person's lack of control over his or her own life. People were dominated politically by the elite classes and economically by their bosses; they were estranged from meaningful relations with their fellow beings by factory discipline and impersonal city life. The anarchists agreed with socialists that people were exploited by the bourgeois capitalist order, but they saw the crux of the problem as not economic but political and spiritual, in terms of domination. The human essence was to be free, to be self-determining, self-conscious, self-motivating. This essence was being denied by all the forces of growth and centralization, by the very scale of modern civilization: big cities, big factories, big states. People could interact in human terms only on the immediate scale of the farm or the workshop, the village or small city (called the *commune* in France). Anarchists longed for a human scale and saw only the inhuman, longed for a natural social order and saw artifice, longed for immediacy and direct control and saw politics mediated through the abstract institutions of the state, whether monarchic or democratic.

Anarchists felt themselves to be fundamentally at odds with modernity. Yet they were not reactionaries seeking to turn back the clock. Although they rejected the present, they were also critical of much of the past, particularly of the power structures of the aristocratic elites and the church. Anarchists had been deeply affected by the radical critique of traditional European values and power made during the Enlightenment. They therefore looked to the future, not to the past—but their vision of the future resembled the past more than the present: a past shorn of elites, domination, and religion, composed of free peasants and artisans reaping the fruits of their own labors. Anarchists were *revolutionaries* in the original sense of the term: rather than believing in the limitless progress proclaimed by liberals or the determinist dialectic of history envisioned by Marxists, they wished to "revolve" back to a more harmonious society. The anarchist rejection of contemporary society was nearly total; their proposed alternative fused elements of a remembered past with a vision of a utopian future.

The Geography of Anarchism

The image of anarchist nostalgia for a simpler past would seem to agree with the Marxist notion of anarchists as "primitive rebels" who lashed out blindly and ineffectually at modernity before being superseded by the progressive forces of socialism. The anarchist movement in the nineteenth century did in fact appeal precisely to those regions and to those social strata that were undergoing rapid modernization and fighting a rear-guard action against being brought into the modern world. Anarchism therefore never took root in industrial England or Germany, nor did it find many recruits among the proletariat courted by the Marxists. Though there were small anarchist movements in the Netherlands and Belgium, it was especially in Latin Europe that anarchists actively and successfully contested with the socialists for the allegiance of the lower classes. Italy, France, and, above all, Spain maintained large artisan and peasant sectors long after these had been submerged in northern Europe. Briefly in the 1870s one of the bastions of anarchist support was in the Swiss Jura, among the skilled watchmakers, but by the 1890s watches were being assembled in factories, and Swiss anarchism was already a memory. Watchmakers, to be sure, hardly deserve to be called "primitive," yet insofar as their conditions of work were independent rather than industrial, they typified preindustrial labor. They had a stake in the past, yearned for a just future, and were fiercely proud of their autonomy. They were anarchists.

In their competition with socialists for followers, anarchists did best recruiting among those sectors of society scorned by Marx as *lumpenproletariat* or as archaic and even reactionary elements. As Marx cursed the idiocy of rural life, thousands of Andalusian peasants flocked to the black flag of anarchy. Anarchism attracted some criminals, prostitutes, hobos, and other socially marginal elements, but mostly it appealed to such workers as cobblers, printers, carpenters, and those engaged in the building trades. Around the turn of the century when anarchists began organizing workers into unions, they still tended to appeal to those with skilled trades rooted in tradition or else to those laboring in largely preindustrial settings, such as lumberjacks and miners in the American West. They were not so much the "have-nots" as the "left-outs" of society.

If the above generalizations are true, then it would seem that anarchism was indeed a movement fated to disappear as the modern industrial world eroded its bases of support. What could be more utopian than to found a revolutionary movement among such obsolete social groups as peasants, craftsmen, and outlaws? By the early twentieth century, the socialists would be surer than ever of the correctness of Marx's version of historical progress, as they enrolled millions in socialist unions and marched them to polling places to elect more and more socialist deputies. Around 1912, it seemed only a matter of time before socialism would triumph through peaceful evolution, while the anarchists and syndicalists who organized workers in anarchist unions raged helplessly below, resorting now to terrorism, now to the new nostrum of the general strike, both fruitless efforts when pitted against the forces of the modern state. And yet socialism did not come to Western Europe as Marx predicted; instead, socialist deputies became increasingly moderate and bourgeois and spoke of improving workers' conditions rather than seizing the means of production. Socialist revolution, when it came in the twentieth century, came to primitive Russia, to China and to Cuba and to Nicaragua, none of which fit the Marxist model. Peasants, declassed urban intellectuals, outlaws, and socially marginal elements could indeed make revolutions. As the workers became integrated into modern, industrial society they lost their revolutionary impetus.

The revolutionary movements of the Third World were not led by anarchists. Only in Spain did anarchists come close to carrying off a revolution, and there they were crushed by more highly organized and better-funded forces, both communist and fascist. However, even though anarchists were not very effective revolutionaries, their analysis of revolutionary potential was in many ways more accurate than the socialists'.

Social and geographical biases are difficult to separate from the temporal attitudes of anarchism. If anarchism was to some degree a revolution of backwardness, it was because social elements that were increasingly archaic in nineteenth-century terms were looking nostalgically back to earlier models of social relations that they deemed less hierarchical, exploitive, and alienating. Marxists had a stake in the present, for only by building on the present could they move forward to the workers' state of the future. And socialists and anarchists alike proclaimed themselves internationalists—antimilitarists who vowed that the only war of the future would be the class war.

Yet nationalism was one of Marx's greatest blindspots, a sentiment whose hold on the popular mind he vastly underestimated. Marx deemed that the economic relations of production were all that really mattered; the state could be theoretically wished away. (In practice, socialist deputies in France and Germany participated increasingly in legislative activity, eventually voting for war credits in 1914.) To anarchists, the state outranked the factory as the essence of the modern malaise. Government, with all its forces of coercion—tax collectors, police, courts, schools, compulsory military service—was the greatest single force constraining the freedom of the individual. If Marxism arose in the midnineteenth century as a protest against the abuses of laissez-faire capitalism, anarchism arose at the same time in opposition to the tremendous currents of nationalism and the rising power of the state. Anarchism conjoined criticism of capitalism, industrialization, and nationalism, going much further than Marxist socialism. That is why anarchists resisted the blandishments offered by the state more than the socialists did, and why they were repressed more severely by the authorities—including the socialist and communist authorities of this century. For anarchists, authority itself was the problem.

The Midnineteenth-Century Origins of Anarchism

The rise of modern anarchism was directly related to the concurrent rise of nationalism, in particular the authoritarian mass nationalism prevalent in Europe after 1848. While a variety of socialist thinkers were grappling with the problems apparent in laissez-faire capitalism in the decades between Napoleon's defeat at Waterloo and the revolutions of 1848, anarchism did not take shape until the years between 1848 and 1871. True, there were a few precursors, such as William Godwin in England, who achieved some fame in the 1790s, and Max Stirner of Germany, who published *The Ego and Its Own* in 1845 but remained entirely unknown until the book was rediscovered in the 1890s. More significantly, the real founder of anarchism, the Frenchman Pierre-Joseph Proudhon, wrote his infamous pamphlet *What Is Property?* in 1840 and shocked Parisians with his straightforward response that property is theft. Yet Proudhon's ideas remained in flux until the 1850s. After the 1848 revolution he actually served in the National Assembly, albeit somewhat unwillingly. The following year he wrote a diatribe against the newly elected president of the Second Republic, Louis-Napoleon Bonaparte, for which he spent the next three years in prison. It was only after his revolutionary disillusionment and imprisonment that he composed his philosophy. Similarly, Mikhail Bakunin was a lifelong revolutionary yet did not really become an anarchist until the 1860s, after he too had endured time in prison and exile in Siberia for his part in the 1848 revolutions. The last great father of modern anarchism, Peter Kropotkin, a generation younger than Proudhon and Bakunin, became an anarchist in the early 1870s, and he too experienced the inside of a prison, first in Russia and later in France. His disillusionment came not over the failed revolutions of 1848 but over the reversal of the brief era of reform carried out by Czar Alexander II in the early 1860s.

By the 1860s, the era of liberal, even revolutionary nationalism was over (except for suppressed nationalities such as Ireland and Poland). The principle of centralized nation-states—in the era of the Second Reich in Germany and of unified, monarchical Italy—reigned supreme. Anarchism arose in opposition to the international anarchy of the warring, competitive states of the midnineteenth century. Against the policies enshrined in the term *Realpolitik* (the politics of realism) and embodied in Chancellor Otto von Bismarck, anarchists offered their remedies of small-scale production, grass-roots democracy, and localized control.

Anarchists versus Socialists

If anarchism was a political ideology that rejected politics, it was also a revolutionary movement that rejected revolution. Part of what separated anarchists from socialists was their strikingly different evaluation of the heritage of the age of revolution that had lasted from the late eighteenth century through 1848–49. To Marxists they had been bourgeois revolutions, to be imitated and succeeded by the socialist revolutions of the future. The triumphant capitalist classes were creating their own nemesis in the proletariat and so were doomed, yet Marx accepted the parliamentary states they created to protect their wealth as natural expressions of their accession to power. Anarchists could exult in the insurrectionary fervor of the French Revolution too; the ever-optimistic Kropotkin especially praised it for releasing the forces of the people. Yet the anarchists remembered that despite the activism of the Parisian sections and the federalism of the provinces, what had triumphed in the French Revolution was the authoritarian centralism of the Jacobins, the rule of Robespierre and his Committee of Public Safety, followed by the corrupt Directory and that ultimate usurper of the people's revolution, Napoleon. The people had revolted for liberty and equality, and instead had gotten endless warfare and a police state that was far more centralized than was ever dreamed of by the Sun King, Louis XIV. This same critique of state centralization was being made in the 1850s by the liberal Alexis de Tocqueville, who feared that if one great revolution might establish the foundations of liberty, successive revolutions made any stable government impossible. The anarchists drew a different conclusion. Revolutions, insofar as they were political seizures of power, only passed power into the hands of new elites, who were inevitably corrupted by its touch. After the failures of 1848, anarchists no longer believed in political revolution; in fact, it was precisely those failures that led them to coalesce their ideas along anarchist lines.

Herein lies another apparent paradox. The Marxists tended to ignore the role of the state, in theory, while placing faith in the revolutionary seizure of state power and the consolidation of the workers' state in its place. The anarchists abominated government, yet refused to countenance a direct assault on the hated state. Anarchists hoped to make the services of the state redundant by performing them themselves. People needed to form alternative communities, businesses, schools, newspapers, cafés, marriages, libraries, and so on that were nonhierarchical, nondominative, nonexploitive. In a negative sense the anarchist doctrine might imply sabotaging the boss's factory or not paying rent to the landlord; in a positive sense, anarchists wished to form mutual aid societies and credit banks, personal relationships that could be terminated by mutual consent, schools featuring what anarchists liked to call "integral education" of both manual and intellectual skills. The anarchists tended to believe that a change in attitudes must precede any large-scale social transformation. Power-mad people would simply institute new regimes of power. To destroy rather than replace relations of power, new anarchistic values had to predominate. Given the difficulty of creating a sufficient mass of free people who could then create a free society, it is not surprising that a number of impatient anarchists sought to short-circuit this route by immediate attacks on the state.

Terrorism

The successful attack on Czar Alexander II in 1881 inspired many anarchists to declare all-out war on heads of state and other symbols of power. At their Congress of London, held soon after the czar's assassination, anarchists officially advocated the doctrine known as propaganda by the deed, which acknowledged that a dramatic deed could have more impact on the populace than thousands of earnest pamphlets, and that all means were valid that hastened the onset of social revolution. They never believed that such deeds in themselves would succeed in toppling states, but rather that they might catalyze the masses, undermine the sanctity and inviolability of authority, and so lead to insurrection. Such deeds, furthermore, were to be accomplished by individuals or by small groups, which highlighted the voluntary nature of anarchism; popular revolutionary will, not deterministic historical laws, could change history.

Despite the focus on the propagandistic rather than instrumental value of these attacks on authority, anarchist sanction of what we would now call terrorism was disastrous for the movement. Anarchists were equated in the popular imagination with nihilists, who delighted in blind destruction. Bakunin's epigram, "the passion for destruction is a creative passion" was recalled, and writers as distinguished as Joseph Conrad, G. K. Chesterton, Emile Zola, and Henry James felt compelled to offer the public novels featuring sinister conspirators deploying bombs and daggers to destroy the citadels of power.[1] Governments across Europe closed anarchist newspapers and arrested as many militants as they could, while the terrorists were executed by noose, garrote, and guillotine. The mostly parliamentary socialists of the turn of the century fell over each other trying to distance themselves from the anarchists, and expelled them definitively in 1896 from their Congress of London.

Three years later Alexandre Millerand became the first socialist deputy in Europe to accept a ministerial portfolio, thereby becoming part of the government rather than sitting with the vocal opposition. The anarchists went their own way.

But what way? Individual deeds were stirring but ineffectual and marked anarchism with a negative image it has never erased. Revolution was suspect for its devotion to politics and its exaltation of leaders who would be corrupted by the temptations of power. Spontaneous insurrection was more to the anarchists' liking, implying as it did the direct action of the people, but in the aftermath of government repression of anarchists in the 1890s, they were well aware of the power of the state to put down popular uprisings. There were always social and cultural alternatives: one could organize free schools, write for anarchist newspapers, sing rebellious songs in anarchist cabarets. All these things the anarchists did, but they still sought new methods of attacking the power structure while involving the working masses in anarchist alternatives. The solution from the 1890s to the First World War was anarcho-syndicalism.

Anarcho-syndicalism

Syndicat is simply the French word for union. Unions themselves were legalized in most European states only toward the end of the nineteenth century, by which time there were already socialist unions, Christian unions (usually favored by employers for their docility), and some nonpolitical ones. At the height of the terrorist wave, in 1892, some of the most influential international anarchists exiled in London, including Kropotkin, the Italian Errico Malatesta, and the French Louise Michel and Charles Malato, called for anarchist penetration of unions. When the rabble-rousing French publicist Emile Pouget returned from exile in London in 1895, he advocated this tactic in his new paper. Others were similarly addressing the anarchists' greatest liability, their lack of organization. The most effective synthesis of libertarian ideals and organization was provided by Fernand Pelloutier between 1895 and 1901. In the 1890s he founded the Fédération des Bourses du Travail, which were labor exchanges where workers sought jobs and often found anarchist propaganda. Also in 1895 the association of French labor unions, the Confédération Générale du Travail (CGT), was formed. The year after Pelloutier's death in 1901, the CGT united with the

Bourses under the vigorous direction of the anarchist Victor Griffu-elhes. The era of anarcho-syndicalism was born, and the French model was soon to be imitated elsewhere; in Spain for example, the Confederación Nacional de Trabajo (CNT) was formed in 1910.

Syndicalism provided a number of important new directions for the anarchist movement. Most immediately, it substituted more positive tactics and ideals for those of individualistic terrorism. Of greater long-term importance, it suggested that anarchism was a movement willing to come to grips with modernity, able to vie with socialism on its own terrain rather than being romantically tied to the past. A new culture of proletarian solidarity was replacing the older mix of bohemian individualism and illegalism. Instead of propaganda by the deed, the syndicalists adopted the slogan "direct action" as appropriate for the new revolutionary method of the general strike. While not eschewing workplace reforms and better salaries, the anarcho-syndicalists made it clear that their ultimate goal was still revolutionary, and that their means would be economic rather than political. If a large number of workers were organized and on a given day laid down their tools, occupied the factories, and otherwise made the industrial infrastructure grind to a halt, the revolution would be accomplished, the workers would take over the means of production, and the state would, somehow, collapse. Several such general strikes were called, and governments responded vigorously when essential services such as railroads were threatened. French Prime Minister Aristide Briand called out the army to run the trains in 1910, and threatened to draft the strikers.

By 1912 the CGT had 600,000 adherents, a sizable number but still only a fraction of the total workforce necessary to carry out a general strike, and far fewer than were enrolled in the German socialist unions. The socialists denounced the syndicalist general strike as "general nonsense"; they themselves had by this time largely forgone their revolutionary aspirations. Their well-paid socialist union functionaries were on increasingly good terms with the employers, could point to tangible improvements in the workers' conditions, and increasingly resembled the frock-coated socialist deputies in the German Reichstag. The anarchist unions, by contrast, had low dues and virtually no strike funds; their leaders were usually unpaid. Yet they remained activist and antipolitical until the First World War.

One should not exaggerate the contrast between nineteenth-century anarchism and twentieth-century syndicalism. Not all anarchists accepted the new approach; many feared that their autonomy would be compromised by the collective and industrial atmosphere of union and factory. Individualist, bohemian, and even illegalist anarchists remained apart. The most famous of the latter category may have been the Bonnot Gang, a French anarchist band of thieves who were among the first criminals to use getaway cars in their holdups, before they were caught in 1913. In the 1920s the Spanish anarchists Buenaventura Durruti and Francisco Ascaso robbed banks in a number of countries before becoming anarchist heroes and martyrs during the Spanish civil war. The anarchist unions did not appeal to the same workers as the socialists did, either. They had little success among large, highly industrialized enterprises such as textiles. The workshop rather than the large factory, the independently minded building trades, the mining and logging camps of the American West remained the locus of anarchist support. The syndicalists wanted to act on the world more effectively than had the terrorists. They saw no conflict between bettering their immediate lot and bringing down the system in the long term. They retained the anarchist vision of a radically different future, but they were pragmatic revolutionaries.

The heyday of the international anarchist movement was undoubtedly the period from 1880 to 1914. Nationalism, imperialism, and monopoly capitalism coalesced to bring unprecedented power and prosperity to the privileged strata of European and American society. Anarchism represented the most striking negation of all these forces. For with the exception of the little-known Russian social democrats, called Bolsheviks and Mensheviks after 1903, the socialist parties of Europe and America were mostly reformist in this era, leaving the revolutionary terrain to anarchists and anarchosyndicalists. Then the culmination of nationalist rivalries in the First World War, and the Russian Revolution that followed in its wake, administrated a one-two blow from which anarchism never fully recovered. The great exception, Spain, remained neutral during the war, and the rapid industrial growth that the war stimulated there actually encouraged the spread of anarchist unions. When an even more rabid form of militarist nationalism, fascism, took hold, anarchism appeared to succumb. While the anarchists offered visions of natural order and personal freedom, the European masses clamored for the regimented order of uniforms, for obedience to omnipotent leaders, for the absolute security and identity of blood and biology.

Anarchism as a mass movement was broken by the nationalist state on the one hand, and by the communist state on the other.

During the "red scare" that followed the Bolshevik Revolution, anarchists as well as socialists were persecuted in the Western democracies, even before the rise of the radical right. The First World War gave the United States government a rationale for jailing dissidents as well as increasing nativist sentiment; after the war the government began deporting large numbers of anarchist aliens. Emma Goldman and Alexander Berkman were returned to their native Russia, where they were soon joined by American-born Big Bill Haywood, leader of the Industrial Workers of the World (IWW). Many Italian anarchists were sent back to their homeland as well. Anarchists struck back with bombs, including one placed at the home of the attorney general of the United States, A. Mitchell Palmer. In May 1920, two Italian-American anarchists, Nicola Sacco and Bartolomeo Vanzetti, were charged with the deaths of a paymaster and his guard during the robbery of a shoe factory in Massachusetts. When the indictments were handed down in September, an anarchist compatriot responded by parking an explosive-laden horsecart at the corner of Wall and Broad Streets, in the heart of New York's financial district. The bomb went off during the busy lunch hour, killing 33 people and injuring 200 others, making it the worst explosion of its kind in U.S. history, though it failed to achieve the notoriety of the bomb thrown in Haymarket Square in Chicago in 1886. The trial of Sacco and Vanzetti occurred at the height of the red scare, and the verdict that condemned them to death was widely seen as a travesty of impartial justice. While it was more than likely that both men had been involved in the recent spate of bombings, evidence of their involvement in the robbery-murder was inconclusive at best. The worldwide demonstrations protesting their sentence were in vain; they went to the electric chair in 1927.[2]

Despite such repression, and notwithstanding their opposition to all government, anarchists found it easier to operate in liberal democracies than in the one-party states emerging in the inter-war era. Anarchism would reemerge during the Second Republic in Spain, after 1931, and again in the permissive societies of the West in the 1960s. Before studying these developments in more detail, let us return to the origins of anarchism in a time increasingly remote from our own.

2

The Philosophy of Anarchism

Anarchism, as philosophy and movement, was a product of the midnineteenth century. Responding to the loss of individual identity, to the regimentation and domination that seemed to be the hallmarks of the modern age, anarchists attacked capitalism, industrialization, and the state. Anarchists managed to find nearly all of the dominant political and economic trends of the era wanting. Soon they were warning of the danger to the individual posed by authoritarian, bureaucratic socialism. Did their radically different ideas emerge sui generis, in response to the rapidly changing social and political environment, or could anarchists be drawing on a heritage of libertarian thought? Was there any figure in the development of anarchist ideas comparable to Karl Marx in the socialist camp or, true to their refractory temperaments, did anarchists reject all moves toward doctrinal orthodoxy and intellectual domination?

Enlightenment Origins

The philosophy of anarchism was uniquely a nineteenth-century creation, yet it did not emerge in an intellectual vacuum. The thought of Pierre-Joseph Proudhon and Peter Kropotkin derived directly from the ideas of the eighteenth-century Enlightenment. Their spiritual forefathers were the philosophes Jean-Jacques Rousseau and Denis Diderot, the Marquis de Condorcet and William

Godwin. Mikhail Bakunin and, later, Gustav Landauer can more easily be placed in the Romantic tradition, but even they depended on the philosophes' belief in the perfectability of humanity. Anarchy, order without domination, represented in their minds the furthest stage in humanity's march toward self-perfection. Without such enlightened optimism concerning humanity's fundamental rationality and goodness, and the possibility of social change, anarchists could scarcely have envisioned their stateless utopia, and perhaps would have turned instead to atavistic attacks on all symbols of progress.

The one philosopher who is often cited as an important anarchist thinker and yet who does not fit this mold, Max Stirner, may in fact not deserve the anarchist appellation. Stirner formed his ideas in a violent reaction against the Hegelian and neo-Hegelian versions of Enlightenment rationalism. In considering his extreme individualist form of anarchism or, perhaps better, nihilism, we will require a brief excursion into the Hegelian matrix that shaped the ideas not only of Stirner but also of Bakunin and Proudhon (as well, of course, of Marx) in the 1830s and 1840s. Before we encounter Hegel and his famously disloyal followers, we must survey the Enlightenment origins of all subsequent libertarian thought.

First the necessary disclaimer: neither Rousseau nor Diderot were anarchists, or even revolutionaries. Rousseau has been called many things, among them the "father of totalitarian democracy," yet his radical insights into man's nature are essential baggage for all anarchist travelers. Rousseau went the furthest of the philosophes in controverting the church's teaching that man was fundamentally sinful, and in popularizing the opposite notion that people were naturally good and were only corrupted by society. A Genevan, Rousseau had much the same negative reaction to Parisian society that Proudhon later had when he arrived there from Besançon: luxury and artifice killed the natural goodness they found in simple peasants and artisans. Great cities, wealth, and power were all inimical to goodness. Rousseau, like Proudhon, was a moralist, and though his conclusions differed from Proudhon's in their political implications, the starting point was identical: modernity, in its urban and elite guise, did not promote goodness. Further, in his *Discourse on the Origin of Inequality* Rousseau traced the origins of man's fall from grace to private property and inequality of wealth. Like many of the philosophes, Rousseau idealized societies that appeared uncorrupted by wealth and egoism, such as those of the American

Indians. Far from being benighted heathens, non-European tribal peoples came to be seen as noble savages, founts of virtue living close to nature and, thus, to their own human natures as well.

Eighteenth-century primitivism was thus based on replacing traditional Christian beliefs with those of a new deity, Nature. Anarchists accepted this fundamental transvaluation in which that which was natural was seen as good, and also as rational. Although Rousseau and Diderot idealized the Huron Indians and the Tahitians, they were not true primitivists seeking to return Europeans to some simpler pastoral existence. Rather, erecting Nature as norm gave them a powerful perspective from which to level attacks on their own society. Once people believed that there were just, rational, natural laws that demanded obedience, then civil and religious laws could be compared and found wanting. This is just what Diderot did in his primitivist essay *Supplement to the Voyage of Bougainville* (1772), in which the Tahitian native Orou debates the European-Christian ship's chaplain, and shows himself to be at once more rational, moral, and sensuous, a model of the happy, unrepressed being. The fruits of the chaplain's morality are hypocrisy and guilt; civil law creates the very crimes it punishes. Orou may not have been an anthropologically convincing Tahitian, but he was an effective mouthpiece through which Diderot could heap scorn on contemporary mores and simultaneously present a nobler alternative.

Atheist or deist philosophes used natural-law rhetoric to criticize civil society, the church, and the polity, much as the anarchists would a century later. This discourse also implicitly sanctioned the freedom of the individual. Man in the state of nature was free; limitations on his freedom were conditional and revocable (an idea made popular in John Locke's contract theory of government). Rational men had no need of arbitrary laws imposed from the outside. True laws were engraved on each person's heart, as Rousseau said; one had only to look within. This suggests that natural-law theory sanctions individualism, insofar as truth is to be found in a person's own desires rather than in corrupted institutions. The overriding goal of most Enlightenment philosophes was to attain the greatest possible freedom for individual expression and thought, so people might gain more knowledge of the world and achieve a more perfect society.

Enlightened social thinking left a dual legacy. Natural-law theory, with its built-in distrust of institutions, led to liberalism and to anarchism. On the other hand, the utilitarianism of Jeremy Bentham, with its democratic-rationalist formula of "the greatest happiness of the greatest number," led to the welfare state and to socialism. Freedom for the first, equality and "happiness" for the second— these were the diverging goals of Enlightenment thought. One of Marx's famous dicta was that man has no nature, only history. Progress entails social engineering. Where anarchists sought harmony with nature, Marxists used metaphors of command and control, and had no use for back-to-nature movements. Marxists scoffed at anarchist naïveté concerning human nature and were closer to a Lockeian, sensationalist view of man as plastic, ready to be molded by a new, improved society. The anarchists replied that they did not place unlimited faith in men; that was why they preferred not to entrust any individual with too much power. Still, the ideal of natural harmony, together with its primordial associations, remained a potent anarchist myth. Where Marxists trusted teleology, anarchists looked back to origins.

It is not surprising that the philosophes saw Old Regime governments as a hindrance to the free use of reason. Yet these revolutionary doctrines were not propounded by revolutionaries, nor by anarchists; many philosophes would have been quite content with a rational dictator who took advice from men like themselves rather than from noblemen and the church. Despite all the scorn they heaped on the particular *form* the state took, few philosophes condemned the state as such, but rather hoped to bring it more in line with natural law. Central to Enlightenment political theory was the notion of a contract in which people traded some of their primordial liberty for a measure of security. Since liberal forefather John Locke considered the possession of property to be an inalienable right, for example, it was worthwhile to cooperate with a government that safeguarded that particular right. Such compromises for the sake of private property clearly would not do for an anarchist, and at least one true anarchist emerged in the eighteenth century who said as much.

That dissenter was William Godwin, whose *Enquiry Concerning Political Justice* sold several thousand copies and made him famous in his time, though his fame faded quickly and he left no anarchist movement in his wake. Godwin was born in England in 1756; his minister father intended that his son follow him in his spiritual calling. Godwin's encounter with religion, however, turned him into an atheist. Nevertheless, a Calvinist, puritanical streak remained in his writings. His anarchist utopia demanded moral seriousness and self-restraint.[1]

Godwin's book was published in 1793, during the Jacobin Reign of Terror, and he was seen in England as being a great proponent of the French Revolution, yet Godwin was neither a revolutionary nor a supporter of Robespierre. He was actually much closer to the liberal Condorcet in his belief in the Enlightenment ideal of human perfectability through reason. Like so many thinkers of his day, he saw religion, unreason, the state, and private property as hindering the creation of a just society; unlike the others, he advocated abolishing them. To Godwin it seemed fundamentally unfair to bind all succeeding generations to a contract made by one's hypothetical ancestors. Nor was such a situation necessary; so great was Godwin's faith in human reason that he believed once injustice was abolished, noncoercive cooperation would be guaranteed. In his egalitarian utopia, people would cooperate because they were naturally sociable. Marriage, too, would be abolished, replaced by free mutuality, even though Godwin was himself married twice, the first time to Mary Wollstonecraft, who shared his ideas about equality between the sexes. Violence would not be necessary nor even sufficient to bring this utopia into being; education and rational principles must create anarchists before anarchy itself would be realizable.

Godwin never used the term *anarchism* as a positive noun; perhaps of all the anarchist thinkers, he deserves most to be called a utopian for the perfect rationality of his conception of humanity and society.[2] When all people were educated and rational, he believed, all would be virtuous and all forms of external constraint, superfluous. His secular utopianism was entirely shorn of the messianic fervor that characterized the later anarchist movement. The brooding and conspiratorial figure of Bakunin stands in striking contrast to the serene Godwin.

The Young Hegelians

The supreme exponent of the belief that reality was itself rational and amenable to rational interpretation was Georg Wilhelm Friedrich Hegel, whose life spanned the end of the Enlightenment and most of the Romantic era. Hegel differed from his Enlightenment predecessors in thinking in developmental and historical terms. He was the most powerful exemplar of the historicist cast of mind, which claimed to see purpose in history. For Hegel the idealist, that purpose was defined as the progress of the consciousness of freedom. History was not a series of random events, but the march of Spirit or God toward consciousness, self-consciousness, and, ultimately, toward reason. This sounds tremendously abstract—and it was—but it was concretized for Hegel in the modern Prussian state in which he lived and taught philosophy at the University of Berlin from 1818 until his death in 1831. The modern state, epitomized in Prussia, was deemed by Hegel to most fully express universal ethical standards. Hegel was to the king of Prussia, Friedrich Wilhelm III, what Bishop Bossuet was to Louis XIV in seventeenth-century France: the spokesman for the divine right of kings, who now represented reason rather than faith. This was a surprising conclusion to the highly critical and cosmopolitan spirit of Enlightenment rationalism, but then Hegel was writing after the French Revolution had dramatized the risks of reason, and after Napoleon had sparked the spirit of German nationalism. Of course Hegel was arguing for the *Rechtstaat* or rule of law rather than for the king's personal rule, but in either case there was no sanction for popular revolt as there had been in France or earlier in England. Hegel's dialectic or conflict model of progress culminated in an ideology of social reconciliation, if not for the philosopher himself, for the Prussian authorities who welcomed his philosophy as the ideal academic justification of their rule. How ironic, then, that within a decade of the great philosopher's death, Hegelianism was spawning dangerous radical ideas that would be locked in mortal combat with the new nationalist ethos.[3]

Of all the Young Hegelians who were inspired by the master's method but found his conclusions wanting, Karl Marx became the most influential. In the 1840s, however, he was still overshadowed by Ludwig Feuerbach and, for a short time in 1844 and 1845, by the most iconoclastic of all of Hegel's erstwhile disciples, Max Stirner. Feuerbach led the way in turning Hegel over on his head—or, as Marx later put it, standing him up on his feet. While preserving Hegel's historicism and his dialectical method of understanding historical change, the Young Hegelians saw this change in material rather than ideational terms. Where Hegel saw Providence working out a divine plan, Feuerbach substituted a wholly materialistic interpretation of the march toward human perfection. He declared in *The Essence of Christianity* (1841) that religion led to man's alienation from himself. Theology must be replaced by anthropology, he said, if man, overcoming the sense that he is sinful and flawed, is to stop projecting all of his own positive attributes onto God and instead make himself godlike. Marx was tremendously inspired by Feuerbach's humanism, but critized him for not going far enough. It was not enough to speak of Man; one should look to particular human beings in their actual social and economic relations with one another. Applying the dialectic to the continuing class struggle throughout history, Marx announced that the industrial proletariat would inherit the earth, eventually and inevitably replacing the bourgeoisie as the dominant class, as socialism replaced capitalism and private property was abolished.

Max Stirner

There was a group of Young Hegelians who met regularly at a Berlin wine cellar in the early 1840s and called themselves *die Freien,* the Free Men. Marx and Engels occasionally attended the discussions at Hippel's Weinstube, where the renegade theologian Bruno Bauer presided. Among the inner circle of regulars in this group was Max Stirner. Born Johann Caspar Schmidt in Bayreuth, Bavaria, in 1806, the same turbulent year that Napoleon formally abolished the Holy Roman Empire, Stirner received his literary pseudonym as a nickname referring to his broad forehead. Of lower-middle-class origins, he managed to attend the local classical Gymnasium, and went on to the University of Berlin, where, between 1826 and 1828, he heard lectures by Hegel himself on the history of philosophy. Stirner hoped to obtain a teaching position at a Gymnasium, but he did not do well on his oral examinations and had to settle for a job teaching history and literature at a Berlin girls' school.[4] This unlikely setting provided him the financial security to associate with the freethinkers at Hippel's and to compose, in 1844, his one major philosophical contribution. This book, *Der Einzige und sein Eigenthum,* appeared at almost exactly the moment that Friedrich Nietzsche was being born about a hundred miles away, near Leipzig.[5] The two philosophers' names are frequently linked, since both achieved fame at the same time, in the 1890s, and both have been seen as proto-existentialists or, as one commentator styles them, as anarcho-psychologists.

Stirner's book is usually translated as *The Ego and Its Own,* but this is only an approximation of the German, which might better be rendered "The Unique One and His Property." Like Nietzsche's Overman, Stirner's Unique One rises above the herd, above laws and socially and morally imposed limitations. He is the self-created being who, to define himself, must attack all the forces of modern society that seek to repress the free individual. Unlike Nietzsche, Stirner composed his attack on all truths in the heyday of the Young Hegelians. His fellow freethinkers attacked religion in the name of humanity. Stirner went further, arguing that a true atheist must renounce all beliefs, including those secularized versions of religious faith to which the Young Hegelians subscribed, whether Humanity, Society, or the Proletariat. He states in the introduction to his book, "Nothing is more to me than myself," and after dissecting and, we might now say, deconstructing all contemporary forms of liberal political and social thought, concludes, "I have made Nothing my cause."[6] Throughout the book he repeats his nihilistic credo: "Away with every cause which is not wholly and entirely my cause! Do you think that my cause must at least be "the good cause"? Good and evil indeed. I am my own cause, and I am neither good nor evil. . . . My cause is neither the divine nor the human, it is not the true, the good, the just, or the free cause, but simply *mine*, and it is not anything general, for it is—*unique*, as I am unique. Nothing is more to me than myself!"[7]

All causes and ideals function, as does religion, to deny the self. Stirner's egoistic individual exists without extension in either time or space; he denies progress toward some great goal as well as commitment to some cause. Nothing is left, not even belief in individualism; the ego merely exists to enjoy and ultimately to dissolve itself.

Stirner's biographer credits him with playing a fundamental role in the development of Marx's scientific socialism. In 1845 Marx labored mightily to refute Stirner's devastating critique of Young Hegelian humanism, since it impugned his own position. Most of his book *The German Ideology* was devoted to attacking Stirner, and although it remained an unpublished manuscript until the twentieth century, it stimulated Marx to reject his early devotion to abstract humanist ideals and base himself instead on objective economic and sociological reality. As for Stirner, Marx predictably characterized him as a petit bourgeois intellectual divorced from social reality, encased in a world of self-supporting categories that led to the purest solipsism.[8] He might have quoted King Lear to the effect that "nothing comes of nothing."

Nihilist, psychologist, proto-existentialist; but was Max Stirner an anarchist? Not in the sense that the other thinkers being discussed in this chapter deserve the term. Certainly, unlike Proudhon, Bakunin, and Kropotkin, he never applied the word to himself. Engels much later suggested that Bakunin studied Stirner's thought and even blended him with Proudhon to create anarchism, but his statements were based on no evidence. In the 1890s a German poet named John Henry MacKay rediscovered the long-forgotten philosopher, and he became popular along with Nietzsche among the artists and aesthetes who flocked to anarchism at the end of the nineteenth century. Since then, most histories of anarchism have included Stirner under the rubric "individualist anarchist." It is not hard to see why Stirner appealed to individualist anarchists. He attacked much of what they attacked: religion, the state, the family, laws all had no meaning for him. Stirner wrote at one point, "the egoist, to whom nothing is sacred, is by his very existence the most tireless, the most important criminal."[9] This sounded promising to the propagandists of the deed. What is absolutely lacking is the ideal of social regeneration common to all anarchists. Nor would Stirner have accepted the anarchist belief in natural law, the faith that people are naturally sociable and can get along together harmoniously. His nihilist vision is closer to the Hobbesian war of all against all than it is to the anarchist ideal of mutual aid. Such asocial thought that demystified all ideologies but left little in their place disturbed the mystical German anarchist Gustav Landauer, who protested that notions of community and humanity were as real as the individual, and that in fact there was no absolutely independent individual shorn of larger, organic links with his fellow beings.[10] Even if Stirner did not "believe in" freedom any more than other abstractions, his Unique One remained for some an existential alternative to the domination and repression that they believed characterized society. Neither Nietzsche nor Stirner deserve to be called anarchists, yet their thought proved stimulating to many who cherished individuality.

Pierre-Joseph Proudhon

William Godwin was a pure intellectual who never worked at anything other than his writing. Stirner taught in a Berlin school for young ladies, and he, like Godwin, remained unconnected with any social or political movement. The true father of anarchism, the Frenchman Pierre-Joseph Proudhon, was himself a product of the lower classes whose cause he championed. His Franche-Comté forebears had been peasants; his father, an artisan who had achieved a tenuous lower-middle-class status as an innkeeper and brewer (the family remained poor). Despite his forays into Parisian politics and his copious writing, Proudhon remained a peasant at heart who identified with the most traditional segments of society. Like Rousseau, he was a moralist who condemned the corrupt ways of the modern world as exemplified by Parisian society. In fact his career parallels that of Rousseau, who launched his reputation in 1750 by winning an essay contest sponsored by the Academy of Dijon on the topic of whether modern society improved or weakened morals. (Rousseau took the latter viewpoint.) Proudhon won a scholarship to study in Paris from the Academy of his native Besançon, and he established his reputation with his book dedicated to that academy, *What Is Property?*, published ninety years after Rousseau's famous essay. Rousseau attacked modernity; Proudhon did the same—modernity in the guise of the modern state, capitalism, and industry. For both the Geneva watchmaker's son and the Besançon cooper's son, Paris embodied the alienation and hypocrisy that typified urban society. Like so many later populists, they idealized small-town values, and both turned their nostalgia to powerful philosophical uses.

In fact, in all the twenty-six volumes of Proudhon's complete writings and the fourteen additional volumes of his correspondence, Rousseau is the thinker mentioned most frequently.[11] Yet despite his identification with the great philosophe as social critic and moralist, Proudhon was sharply critical of the solutions Rousseau proposed to remedy the ills he witnessed. Proudhon attacked Rousseau's *Social Contract* for dwelling entirely on political solutions while ignoring economic forces. Rousseau's ideas bore perfect testimony to Proudhon's belief that government is the problem, never the solution. The general will posited by Rousseau would only lead to tyranny and the suppression of individual will, as demonstrated by the historical experience of Robespierre in the French Revolution.

Proudhon's rejection of Rousseau did not stop with his critique of what J. L. Talmon later called "totalitarian democracy," however; he also reproached Rousseau for substituting a cult of the emotions for one of reason, thereby endangering the forward march of progress. Proudhon attacked the "Romantic" Rousseau in much the same terms as did such eighteenth-century philosophes as Voltaire, justifying Metternich's description of Proudhon as the illegitimate child of the Encyclopedists.[12] Yet for Proudhon his attack on Rousseau assumed moral as much as philosophical proportions, as he complained that a feminized culture of feelings would undermine masculine rationality and thereby forestall social and intellectual progress. He thought the sentimental Rousseau of *La Nouvelle Héloise* was just as decadent as the elite society that he criticized and that lionized him as the "child of nature." Proudhon perhaps most resembled Rousseau in the ambivalent and contradictory nature of his thought.

Nevertheless, like the Enlightenment philosophes, Proudhon believed deeply in progress, which he defined as the march from authority to liberty and which was synonymous with the progress of man's reason from the shackles of mystery. Religion had always served to buttress authority—all kings ruled ultimately by divine right—so freedom from external authority also implied freedom from religion. The reign of reason and liberty was based on the end of servility to church and state. While he would have been perfectly content with Hegel's definition of history as marking the progress of the self-consciousness of freedom, he would have denied that that progress was in any way identified with the modern state. Proudhon saw freedom as being everywhere constrained by the growth of large, centralized states. This progressive thinker identified true freedom with peasants and artisans, the very groups Marx stigmatized as being retrograde classes that stood in the way of progress. Like Marx, Proudhon saw progress in economic rather than political terms; unlike Marx, he defined progress in terms of the workers' autonomy rather than their economic equality. If history recorded the movement of freedom, the future belonged not to the regimented industrial proletariat but to the proudly independent artisan and farmer, freed from the oppression and interference of kings and bureaucrats. Yet was Marx not right in deeming peasants and artisans to be economically obsolete? And was not Proudhon similarly bucking progress by protesting the development of the centralized nation-state? The anarchist's reading of history was at the least idiosyncratic.

Proudhon was the forerunner as well as the intellectual progenitor of many later anarchists. He was self-educated, trained to be a printer, a trade that required literacy and that produced many staunchly independent autodidacts. Unlike virtually all other major socialist and anarchist thinkers, Proudhon could point proudly to his working-class origins. Anarchists especially distrusted bourgeois theoreticians who claimed to think for the workers, as well as abstract theorizing removed from working-class experience. Proudhon possessed inherent credibility as a worker-intellectual, and if his ideas were less coherent and more contradictory than those of Marx, one might say, so is life itself. The anarchist movement did not produce many Proudhons who wrote so voluminously, but it did become famous for its staunchly independent, self-taught skilled workers who embodied Proudhon's principles. More than any other radical thinker, Proudhon spoke for the common man. What he demanded for them was a social morality by which each individual was free to think and act for himself.

Proudhon is paradoxical, as well, in being an anarchist who renounced violent revolution as a means of attaining his aims. He became famous through his first book, *What Is Property?*, in which he answered the question succinctly: "Property is theft." Yet he was not a collectivist who advocated the abolition of private property. He supported the peasants' and artisans' control of their own property. What he really condemned was capital, that is, property that was unearned and that contributed to the exploitation of others. His criticism of property has a distinctly moral tone, for Proudhon fervently believed in the value of work and supported the right to property one had accumulated through one's own work. Such property actually buttressed the security of the workers and increased their real independence, rather like Jefferson's ideal of the yeoman farmer. On the other hand, one had no right to property that limited the freedom of others. Proudhon's hatred of large-scale, exploitive capital led to his populist panacea of free credit. During the 1848 revolution he tried to establish a Peoples' Bank that would provide free credit so that the individual could establish his own enterprise without becoming beholden to the capitalists. With open access to capital, small business would thrive, privilege would fade away, and political revolution would become obsolete. No wonder Marx called Proudhon a petit bourgeois.

Proudhon did not, however, envision a society composed only of small entrepreneurs. Rather, he felt that workers must freely join together in associations to promote their economic interests. This would make possible larger enterprises owned and run by the workers themselves. In the 1840s, Proudhon worked and lived for a time in Lyon, France's leading industrial city and a hotbed of socialist ideas. He encountered followers of the utopian communist Etienne Cabet, of Fourier, and of Saint-Simon. The largest group was a secret society of mutualists whose leaders had taken part in the worker uprisings of 1831 and 1834 against the regime of King Louis Philippe. These workers shared Proudhon's frustration with political revolution and his belief in the primacy of social and economic change.[13] In Lyon, Proudhon made contact with a real working-class movement, gained experience of the industrial development that was just beginning in France, and developed his ideas concerning workers' societies.

Proudhon's ideas would long be known as mutualism. The model here too was the workshop, with workers cooperating for their mutual benefit. Rather than pursuing the destructive fantasy of revolution, which only created new masters, Proudhon believed workers should concentrate on serving their own economic interests and that social change would inexorably follow. While Proudhon did not deny the reality of class struggle, he hoped to avoid all-out class war by his principles of mutuality and reciprocity, and with much of the bourgeoisie brought within the mutualist order. As production and consumption became increasingly associated with mutualist associations of workers, the different enterprises would need to be coordinated for the exchange of goods and services. The economy would develop from the ground up, exploitation would cease, and the era of justice, defined as respect for human dignity, would commence.

The year 1848—a great watershed in European history—has often been taken to signify the disillusionment of intellectuals with the Romantic and liberal nationalist ideals of the first half of the nineteenth century. Those ideals never appealed to Proudhon, but he was deeply involved in and disillusioned by the course of the revolutionary events of 1848. Elected to the National Assembly by the workers of Paris in early June, he was caught by surprise when those workers took to the streets later that month to protest the dissolution of the national workshops established by Louis Blanc. After the suppression of the workers in the bloody June Days, Proudhon, the anarchist deputy, was heartily hated by his mostly conservative colleagues in the Assembly. In July, he had the temerity to propose a tax on all rents and interest so that the state could finance free-credit facilities and lower other taxes. After he spoke for three hours in favor of his bill, it was resoundingly defeated by a vote of 693 to 2 (a socialist worker named Greppo was his sole supporter).[14]

After the election of Louis-Napoleon Bonaparte as president of the Second Republic, Proudhon wrote a scathing attack on Bonaparte for which he was sentenced to three years in prison. This sentence was less harsh than the one served on Mikhail Bakunin for his part in the insurrection of Dresden, but it served similarly to disabuse

Proudhon of any possible benefit of government—and it preceded Bonaparte's coup d'état. Proudhon's experience in government made him aware of how even the best-intentioned legislator became cut off from his constituents, and the abolition of the national workshops showed him how much the workers could expect from the state. The whole revolutionary tradition dating from 1789 demonstrated to him the uselessness of politics. The February uprising had been a truly popular revolution, from which the male workers received nothing more tangible than the right to vote. Henceforth they must find a different way to achieve their aims.

Proudhon married in 1848 and found great personal happiness with his wife, Euphrasie, and their daughters. As he wrote scathingly of the moral rot of the Second Empire, he rejoiced in his own family life and valued family along with work as essential parts of a just and moral life. As has already been suggested, Proudhon was no feminist, and his very traditional ideas concerning the role of women in the family have caused problems for later anarchists. Proudhon was neither liberal nor tolerant, and he was full of prejudices against black, Jews, and the English, as well as against women. Proudhon, for example, whose birth and death years correspond exactly to those of Abraham Lincoln, supported the American South's right to secede from the Union, despite its manifestly unfree institution of slavery.

Proudhon's last years before his death in 1865 were not easy ones, as he endured sickness and exile, as well as imprisonment, yet his most important books were written during this time of adversity. These included his 1858 book, *Of Justice in the Revolution and in the Church,* and two works published in the year of his death, *On the Political Capacity of the Working Classes* and *On the Principle of Art and Its Social Destination.* This last book expresses his aesthetic views, championing the realist school of art exemplified by the painting of his close friend, Gustave Courbet. But it is impossible to survey here all of the ideas of this extraordinary and sometimes contradictory thinker; instead I will focus briefly on the theme announced in another book, published in 1863, entitled *The Principle of Federation.*

France's long history of administrative centralization was greatly accentuated by the French Revolution and Napoleon's conquest of power. It was also, in the nineteenth century, a politically volatile country, as revolutions in the capital overthrew the government of the entire country. Proudhon linked centralized power, instability, and compulsive revolutionism together, and he offered an alternative that was both more democratic and more stable. Taking the Swiss confederation as his model (again reminiscent of Rousseau), he called for the acceptance of division and diversity, and for respect for regional autonomy and self-government. He longed to revive the civic ideal of the active citizen as well as the cultural differences peculiar to different regions. He wrote the book shortly after the house of Savoy successfully spearheaded the unification of Italy, which Proudhon opposed, and during the American Civil War, when he consistently favored the secessionist states.

Federalism was the territorial counterpart of the economic doctrine of mutualism. In both cases, Proudhon envisioned loose federations linking regions or associations that would coordinate activities without usurping local autonomy. This principle of federation may strike one as strange coming from an anarchist. Did Proudhon favor no government or local government?[15] It may be useful, therefore, to see federalism as anarchy in a positive sense, as providing the greatest degree of self-government practicable in a diverse and sometimes hostile world. Proudhon saw himself as a realist, and he recognized that the anarchist utopia of no government was probably not feasible. In a world dominated by rapidly expanding nation-states he proposed a counter model of decentralized control and direct democracy. In mutualism and federalism (despite his over-reliance on the panacea of free credit) Proudhon bequeathed to anarchism a positive program, which unfortunately would be overshadowed by the violent revolutionary negation of Mikhail Bakunin.

Mikhail Bakunin

That anarchism could claim as its founders two such contrasting figures as Pierre-Joseph Proudhon and Mikhail Bakunin says a great deal about the lack of doctrinal orthodoxy required of adherents to the movement. Close contemporaries (born in 1814, Bakunin was five years younger than Proudhon, and he died eleven years after him, in 1876), they came from opposite sides of the continent, and from opposite social classes, yet they met in Paris in the 1840s and became friends, discussing ideas heatedly through the night in Proudhon's modest lodgings. When Proudhon, himself imprisoned by Louis-Napoleon, heard about Bakunin's incarceration by Czar Nicholas I, he wrote to Alexander Herzen that he had been weeping over Bakunin's "slow assassination."[16] Both men survived their terms of imprisonment, but with their health impaired, and both died prematurely. Where Engels played a compliant Watson to Marx's Sherlock Holmes, the two anarchists, Proudhon and Bakunin, diverged on many issues, most importantly on revolutionary means.

It is impossible to speak of their ideas divorced from the temperaments and experiences of the two men. If Proudhon epitomized the self-taught worker, Bakunin was the exact opposite, the "superfluous man" made famous by Turgenev, scion of a noble Russian family who never had to work and who was freed to indulge in endless soul-searching and philosophizing. While Proudhon had to be forced into exile in Belgium and spent most of his life in Besançon, Lyon, and Paris, Bakunin was the ultimate rootless intellectual, living in Germany, France, Italy, and Switzerland as well as in his native Russia. Where Proudhon settled down and idealized family life, Bakunin was incapable of such stability. His large appetite for food and drink and his heroic revolutionary demeanor masked inner doubts that probably stemmed from sexual uncertainty. Susan Sontag once divided thinkers into husbands and lovers, the steady solid types and the more exciting if unreliable ones; Bakunin, despite his impotence, would join Rousseau and Nietzsche in the latter category. Marx would join Proudhon in the former.

Bakunin became a devotee first of the thought of Fichte and then of Hegel in the 1830s, and eventually he went to Berlin to drink in Hegelian metaphysics at the source. Here he came under the influence of the Young Hegelians and soon made a political left turn. Proudhon made his mark with his slogan, "Property is theft"; as early as 1842, only two years later, Bakunin penned his famous incendiary line in a German journal, "The passion to destroy is a creative passion." Yet it would not be accurate to call Bakunin an anarchist in the 1840s, despite his meetings with Proudhon. Not until his escape from Siberia in 1861, his return to Europe by way of Civil War America, and his growing conflict with Marx in the late 1860s did he really define himself as an anarchist theorist. Bakunin's anarchist writings all belonged to his last decade, and in contrast to both Marx's and Proudhon's, they took the form of scattered impressions rather than a coherent body of work. His admirers have long maintained that Bakunin was first and foremost an activist rather than a thinker, and indeed his huge frame and shaggy, leonine head were famous symbols of revolution in his own day. Rather like

Garibaldi, Bakunin was a legend in his own time who had to live up to his persona. His detractors maintain that he was neither a coherent thinker nor an activist, but a mystic and millenarian who projected his dreams of wholeness and belonging onto the people, and who endlessly fantasized about conspiracies and insurrections with himself at their head.[17] In either or both cases he represents the demonic underside of Proudhon's rational approach, the spirit of revolt that destroys before it rebuilds. It is not hard to see why the combative dreamer Bakunin, not the quiet rationalist Proudhon, captured the imagination of the anarchist movement in the years after 1870.

For Proudhon, history traced a logical continuum from authority to liberty, from the domination of politics to its supersession by social and economic life. In the rational process of history, the anarchist was the most rational of men. The appeal of anarchism for Bakunin was precisely the opposite; it represented the chaos and destruction nearer the commonsense meaning of *anarchy*. For him, anarchism was an instinct for freedom, present in all people. The innate passion of rebellion was most alive in those who were least fettered by the chains of civilization. Bakunin was much more akin to Rousseau than was Proudhon; his noble savages were the peasants, the cossacks of the Russian steppes, outlaws refractory to the orderly demands of the modern world.[18] For quite different reasons, Bakunin idealized artisans and peasants much as Proudhon had, but in addition he thought that socially deviant types, such as criminals, would make good revolutionaries, since they had so little to lose. Unlike the servile proletariat, criminals' spirits had not been broken by the new industrial order. Only such groups could make the revolution, because the type of insurrection Bakunin envisioned had to be spontaneous, an unconstrained outpouring of the natural energy of the people, not the carefully contrived coup d'état of a few professional revolutionaries.[19] Bakunin was a romantic revolutionary to his core. As his revolutionizing preceded his anarchist philosophizing by twenty years, so his fondness for insurrection itself surpassed his hopes for a libertarian society. This is one of Bakunin's key contributions to the movement that emerged after his death, and one that would be picked up by Georges Sorel after the turn of the century in his anarcho-syndicalist *Reflections on Violence:* the cult of revolutionary upheaval and conspiracy. Where Proudhon hoped to avoid revolutionary violence entirely, Bakunin focused on the revolution almost to the exclusion of anything else.

The implications of this revolutionary Rousseauism are profound. If the more backward social elements made better revolutionaries than the industrial proletariat, it stood to reason that revolution was more likely to break out in the less developed regions of Europe, or indeed anywhere that anarchist ideas might be spread and oppression resisted. Such regions were precisely where Bakunin found his greatest support. Though he did not attract much of a following in Russia, he did very well in Italy, France, and, above all, in Spain. (He also for a time found supporters in the mountains of the Swiss Jura, among the independent watchmakers, but this constituency faded by the mid-1880s.) Anarchism differed from Marxism as greatly in its appeal as in its doctrine. Marx of course heaped scorn on "the idiocy of rural life" and referred to the marginal groups Bakunin courted as the *lumpenproletariat*, a hopelessly obsolete group fated to be the reactionary tools of the political elites. With the significant exception of industrial England, Marxist socialism found its strongest bases of support in northern Europe, especially in Germany, and Marx was sure that this was where socialism would triumph.

But Marx was wrong, and the twentieth century has paradoxically supported Bakunin's "unscientific" contention that peasants make good revolutionaries. Countries in the throes of modernization rather than those already fully industrialized have been most prone to class conflict. To the extent that Marxists have acknowledged anarchism's appeal among peasants and artisans, they have seen these potential revolutionaries as engaging in prepolitical, often millenarian forms of revolt. They stigmatize these social groups and anarchism in general as primitive forerunners of the more modern socialist creed. But the history of the late twentieth century has called into question the putative superiority of the Marxist vision, just as the history of the first half of the century has contradicted the Marxist theory of revolution.

Bakunin's contributions to the anarchist revolutionary movement (what the Marxists term *praxis*) rather than to the philosophy of anarchism itself has been emphasized here, because that is where his originality lay. Nevertheless, in the late 1860s he did adumbrate an anarchist reading of history to vie with that of his by then arch rival Karl Marx. Whereas Marx minimized the importance of the state compared to control of the economic means of production, Bakunin saw the growth of political coercion as the major theme of history. He conceived of the early modern state as taking power out of the hands of the Church and the feudal lords, and thus accurately dated the rise of the modern state from the Protestant Reformation rather than from the French Revolution as Marx did.

Like both Marx and Proudhon, Bakunin was a fervent atheist, and probably went further than either of them in condemning Christianity as the greatest enforcer of human submission in history. In the important fragment of his writings published posthumously in 1882 as *God and the State*, Bakunin reiterated the critique of religion made by Feuerbach in 1841, that people endowed God with their own best qualities and debased themselves in his worship. Religion was the essence of alienation. A few passages will amply convey the tone of Bakunin's invective:

> Christianity is precisely the religion par excellence, because it exhibits and manifests, to the fullest extent, the very nature and essence of every religious system, which is the impoverishment, enslavement, and annihilation of humanity for the benefit of divinity. . . . The idea of God implies the abdication of human reason and justice; it is the most decisive negation of human liberty, and necessarily ends in the enslavement of mankind, both in theory and practice. . . . All religions are cruel, all founded on blood; for all rest principally on the idea of sacrifice—that is, on the perpetual immolation of humanity to the insatiable vengeance of divinity. In this bloody mystery man is always the victim, and the priest . . . is the divine executioner.[20]

Though elsewhere he disparaged rational thought for inhibiting the spirit of revolt, in this work Bakunin followed Proudhon in linking reason and revolt in the dual crusade against religion and the state. In place of these despotic authorities, Bakunin counseled obedience to natural laws and to the science that interprets these laws, though he warned against scientists who use their expert knowledge to place themselves in positions of authority. He even proclaimed his adherence to determinism, despite his belief in revolutionary voluntarism and will. Clearly there were discrepancies between Bakunin's roughly sketched thought and his political pronouncements.

Proudhon, Bakunin, Kropotkin, and Marx were all men of their time in acceding to positivist claims of scientific superiority in the quest for truth. Not until the revolt against positivism in the early twentieth century would mystics such as Gustav Landauer and Martin Buber seriously challenge anarchism's basis in science. In most matters of principle, Bakunin followed in Proudhon's footsteps, with the major exception of his attitude toward property. Bakunin was resolutely opposed to all private property and condemned inherited wealth more rigorously even than Marx. Historians often append the term *individualist* to describe Proudhon's anarchism, *collectivist* to Bakunin's, and *communist* to Kropotkin's, as he subscribed to the philosophy of "from each according to his ability, to each according to his needs." One might equally well call Proudhon pragmatic, Bakunin revolutionary, and Kropotkin utopian.

Bakunin shared Marx's sense of the inevitability of social revolution destroying capitalism; he differed sharply from Marx, however, as to the nature and purposes of revolution. These differences from the leader of "scientific socialism" surfaced in the late 1860s as Marx and Bakunin struggled over control of the International Working Men's Association founded by Marx in 1864 to represent the interests of the working class. Initially many of the delegates to the International had been Proudhonian mutualists, but after Proudhon's death Bakunin clearly took charge of the anarchist wing. This wing represented regional as well as ideological differences, the anarchists being strong in Latin Europe, in Switzerland, and to some degree in Holland and Belgium. So great was the threat of anarchist takeover that after Marx managed to have the General Council of the International drum Bakunin and his Swiss supporter James Guillaume out of the organization in 1872, the headquarters was banished to New York City. There the International faded away, not to be revived until 1889, well after Marx's death. The new Second International also struggled against anarchist influence, finally barring all anarchists from its congresses in 1896.

In Bakunin's version of the feud, Marx was an authoritarian German who wanted sole control of the International and who hounded him out over trumped-up charges of revolutionary intrigues. Yet while Bakunin was publicly denouncing the concept of leadership by a revolutionary elite, he was preparing himself and his cohorts for just such a role, creating a series of conspiratorial organizations beholden to him rather than to the International. This was the charge that caused his removal from the organization, and evidence suggests that Bakunin really was engaging in such conspiracies.[21]

How could the spokesman for spontaneous and instinctual mass revolt engage in conspiratorial revolutionary plotting? One answer is that Bakunin was a revolutionary fantasist who dreamed of immense popular uprisings and romanticized the people as being capable of such orgies of destruction, while he also wished to aggrandize his own role in the coming cataclysm to being mastermind of the revolution. In both cases the "superfluous" intellectual overcame his sense of isolation and impotence at the cost of raising the hopes of innocent peasants in fruitless attempts at insurrection.[22] However accurate these attempts at psychological motivation, it is undeniable that Bakunin had a penchant for setting up secret revolutionary organizations during the 1860s. The strangest conspiratorial association of these years was that between Bakunin and the Russian nihilist Sergei Nechaev, a young man of peasant origins and fanatical will for whom the old anarchist had a tremendous fascination. In 1869 in Geneva, they collaborated on the *Catechism of a Revolutionary*, a handbook for ruthless revolutionaries solely dedicated to destruction and terror. The (a)moral code of this work may be summarized in the phrase, "Whatever aids the triumph of the revolution is ethical."[23] The two revolutionaries broke the next year, and it is unclear how much of this notorious work was written by Bakunin, but the affair does reveal both his gullibility and fascination with conspiracy. Nechaev returned to Russia and died in prison in 1882 at the age of thirty-five, after having spent ten years in solitary confinement for the murder of a member of his own revolutionary cell. Nechaevism was completely antithetical to Proudhon's pacific libertarian impulses. If the anarchist credo that authoritarian means cannot lead to libertarian ends has any truth, then there could be no room for the kind of revolutionary elitism dreamed of by Bakunin and Nechaev. The most charitable reading of Bakunin's activities in these years is as foreshadowings of what Spanish anarchists would later call "affinity groups," secret revolutionary cells that could survive periods of repression and encourage mass revolt. Unfortunately Bakunin, like Marx, seemed to retain a lingering taste for a dictatorship of the proletariat—possibly justifiable in a socialist, fatal for an anarchist.

Peter Kropotkin

Proudhon and Bakunin died while anarchism was still in its infancy. Peter Kropotkin, the third great nineteenth-century anarchist thinker, was a generation younger and had the privilege of presiding intellectually over the movement in its heyday, between 1880 and

1914. While he felt duty-bound to take an active role in the movement, his real contribution was not as militant or organizer but as philosopher, in redefining the meaning and direction of anarchism for thousands of adherents and even more thousands of curious people who wanted to understand what lay beneath the violence of the terrible apostles of "propaganda by the deed."

The title "Philosopher" no doubt would have been welcomed by Proudhon, while Bakunin can be described most succinctly as the rebel; Kropotkin would have felt more comfortable with the sobriquet, scientist. Even more of a positivist than his predecessors, he contended that anarchism was a science firmly rooted in natural law and in the modern world. Calling it a science meant rescuing anarchism from the vagaries of metaphysics, utopianism, and random violence, and placing it on a firmer footing. Kropotkin convinced himself that anarchism was in the very nature of things and represented the wave of the future. This scientific aura gave to Kropotkin's writings a tone of benign optimism about anarchism's prospects, which were dubious in an era of increasing nationalism, militarism, and imperialism.

Peter Kropotkin would seem to have been an unlikely candidate for radical politics, belonging as he did to the highest echelons of the Russian aristocracy, but in a century and in a country that had produced three anarchistic aristocrats (Bakunin and Count Leo Tolstoy being the other two), not to mention numerous other well-born radicals, Kropotkin's apostasy from class-based self-interest was clearly deeply rooted. Many members of the Russian elite were growing disenchanted with the reactionary political and social status quo of czarist Russia. Educated to Western European standards, they felt a profound dissonance when they looked at their own startlingly unequal society of privileged elites and servile peasants. Many members of the Russian intelligentsia opted for various forms of revolutionary socialism but, with the exception of Lenin himself, produced no socialist figures of the stature of Bakunin, Kropotkin, and Tolstoy. The really remarkable trait shared by these three members of the Russian elite was their willingness to sacrifice their wealth and social position for their ideals. The benign, bearded Kropotkin was frequently referred to as the anarchist saint for his simple way of life; Tolstoy donned the garb of his serfs. This self-sacrificial behavior exercised a powerful attraction, leading those followers who condoned violence to call the terrorists being put to death "anarchrists," while Tolstoyans practiced a Christian form of anarchist nonviolence.

For Kropotkin, it was disillusionment with the prospects of reform that turned him away from his early scientific interests, toward the cause of the people. Born in 1842, he reached young adulthood during the reform era of Czar Alexander II, the monarch who freed the Russian serfs in 1861 and seemed to promise political reforms as well. Kropotkin was a member of the czar's corps of pages, a position reserved for the highest aristocracy. He received an army commission and was posted to Siberia at a time when it was being integrated into the Russian Empire. The young officer had the opportunity to explore territory previously unknown to the West, and he compiled extensive geographical information.

It is striking that the two leading anarchist thinkers of the late nineteenth century were geographers, the other being the Frenchman Elisée Reclus. One explanation might be that geography in those days included what would now be called cultural anthropology, and both men developed a fine appreciation for cultural diversity, especially among "primitive" peoples being submerged by European expansionism. Anarchist calls for diversity and nondominative relationships perhaps addressed their awareness of the need for greater cultural relativism. Kropotkin reported admiringly from Siberia on the self-sufficiency, equality, and cooperation among some of the peoples he encountered on the Siberian frontier, such as the Doukhobor religious sectarians.[24]

As he was encouraged by what he found at the edge of civilization, he was discouraged by the news coming from home. In 1863 the Poles rose against Russian domination, and Kropotkin attributed the czar's merciless crackdown to a change in the political climate, away from reform. The progressive governors in charge of Siberia were recalled, and Kropotkin felt the weight of centralized bureaucracy and power crushing his youthful hopes for change, as he reported much later in his *Memoirs of a Revolutionist*. In 1871 he was offered the position of secretary to the Russian Royal Geographical Society, but turned it down on the grounds that the delights of pure knowledge must give way to the more immediate needs of social reform. This was the year of the Paris Commune, which transfixed the European left with its brief, heroic life and tragic and bloody suppression. As with so many of the populists and other idealistic young Russians, Kropotkin's efforts for reform landed him in prison. After spending two years in the grim Peter and Paul Fortress in St. Petersburg, he managed to escape 30 June 1876, the day before Bakunin died in Switzerland. He then set sail for Sweden and England; he would not return to his homeland for forty-one years.

Kropotkin spent the next decade in Western Europe, mostly in Switzerland and France, absorbing anarchist ideas and taking an increasingly important role in propagating those ideas. Like Bakunin, he was inspired by the anarchists of the Swiss Jura, and he helped found the newspaper *Le Révolté* in Geneva in 1879, which later moved to Paris and under the name *La Révolte* became one of the leading anarchist organs. He played a major role in the 1881 anarchist Congress of London, which convened soon after the Russian terrorist members of Narodnaya Volya succeeded in assassinating Alexander II. Strongly influenced by this revolutionary success, the anarchists at the congress, including Kropotkin, recommended the doctrine known as propaganda by the deed as an efficacious way of spreading the spirit of revolt among the people. Kropotkin did not conceive of this as necessarily implying individual acts of terror, and though he later had cause to regret his association with terrorism, he never fully renounced the anarchist recourse of violence. In fact, in later years he justified it by saying that all parties resorted to violence in direct proportion to the repression visited upon them by the authorities.

Kropotkin soon gained more personal familiarity with government repression. After a series of disturbances among coal miners at Montceau-les-Mines and some explosions in the city of Lyon, the French government began to round up all the leading anarchists it could find, accusing them of inciting violence and conspiring to bring down the state. Kropotkin was one of a number of anarchist militants condemned at Lyon, and he spent three years in French prisons. Though he had had no hand in planning any dynamite attacks, he was in fact sympathetic to the miners called La Bande noire (The Black Group). The spontaneous, worker-oriented actions of the miners were much closer to Kropotkin's idea of social revolution than was individual terrorism. At the trial he had told the jury that the social revolution was near and predicted it would strike within the next ten years. Some of his colleagues felt this declaration was too restrained and believed that popular revolt was imminent.[25] Upon his release early in 1886 he left for England, where he lived for most of the remainder of his long life in the quiet Hammersmith district of London, in a modest house far removed from the princely

Russian estate of his childhood, with its 1,200 serfs and dozens of servants. It is tempting to put a Hegelian gloss on the roles of these three theorists of anarchism, with Proudhon creating the original thesis in mostly constructive terms, Bakunin playing the violent negator of existing reality, and Kropotkin effecting a synthesis that was affirmative but more radical than Proudhon's tame, individualist approach to anarchism. Coming from the Russian revolutionary tradition, Kropotkin was committed to the necessity of violence and went beyond both Proudhon and Bakunin in advocating what he called anarchist communism. He envisioned a future beyond scarcity; therefore, money and private property would be obsolete. Further, he argued that collectivism only concerned people as producers of wealth, while in fact all people were both producers and consumers and both economic aspects needed to be reorganized cooperatively. As he shed his activist garb and donned the mantle of the elderly saint of anarchism, Kropotkin paid much less attention than had Bakunin to the means of achieving the state of anarchy and concentrated instead on the beatific vision of a society without external constraint, in which the individual would be melded harmoniously with the community. What is remarkable about the great outpouring of writing Kropotkin produced between 1886 and 1914 is that he claimed for his utopia the authority of science.

Kropotkin fell under the dual nineteenth-century spell of positivism and historicism. The former ideology led him to base his social views on their perceived congruence with the laws of nature; the latter led him to claim for anarchism both historical antecedents and the predictive capacity to ascertain an anarchist future. Humanity, he believed, was evolving toward anarchy. This intellectual approach was similar to that also being proffered by Karl Kautsky and the orthodox Marxists: a facile optimism about the historical inevitability of socialism that deemphasized the need to promote revolution actively in the here and now. Kropotkin's fellow anarchist Errico Malatesta protested against precisely this tendency in Kropotkin's thought and argued that anarchism was an aspiration toward an ideal that could not be wholly subsumed within a synthetic philosophy.[26] Others complained about the old man's dogmatic intransigence about other points of view. Though its limitations are today evident, the attempt to create such a synthetic interpretation of natural and historical evolution remains impressive.

Kropotkin had left for Siberia in 1862 with *The Origin of Species* ringing in his ears, but he observed there more natural cooperation than competition. Later he read Kessler's *On the Law of Mutual Aid* and had felt compelled to reply to T. H. Huxley's 1888 article, "The Struggle for Existence," in a series of articles written between 1890 and 1896 and eventually collected under the title *Mutual Aid*. In this work, Kropotkin tried to reverse the entire tenor of Social Darwinism, one of the dominant ideologies of the late nineteenth century, which rationalized capitalism, nationalism, and imperialism as examples of the law of survival of the fittest. Kropotkin protested that animals did not try to maximize their individual survival, but rather that of the species, and often performed acts of great self-abnegation. Arguing that the most adaptive behavior was cooperative not competitive, he predictably concentrated on the behavior of such social animals as ants and bees. He claimed that the principle of voluntary cooperation was similarly basic to human society, and saw the recent trend toward competitive individualism as an aberration.

From his spatial consideration of nature and geography, Kropotkin then turned to anarchist historicism. Whereas virtually all history textbooks of the time dwelled on the rise of the nation-state as *the* theme in modern history, Kropotkin agreed with Bakunin that the centralized state was a comparatively recent product of the Reformation and moreover was already showing signs of decline. He then turned to his archetype of the free community, the medieval cities that had thrived as prosperous and autonomous polities in the eleventh through fourteenth centuries. Not only were the citizens of the city free men, not beholden to any lord, but they cooperated for their economic as well as political benefit. Kropotkin idealized the guilds as humane brotherhoods, the free commune as a masterpiece of economic organization and rich communal culture with no need for the formal bureaucracy of the sprawling modern state. "The Commune is an oath of mutual aid," Kropotkin quoted from a twelth-century document.[27] He also approved of the way in which communes banded together in federations to resist the incursions of kings and emperors. He cited the great prosperity of the twelfth and thirteenth centuries, made possible by these communes, and compared the Gothic art of the era favorably with the Baroque art that glorified kings and popes in the power-mad seventeenth century. Kropotkin saw Gothic architecture as a monument to the collective experience of the people (though not of religion—he downplayed medieval religiosity), the triumph of handicrafts fostered by brotherhood and the union of craftsmen. He could not resist comparing the cathedral with that "meaningless scaffold . . . the Paris iron tower."

Kropotkin blamed the decline of the free commune in the sixteenth century on internal class divisiveness, as burghers saw their interests diverge from those of the common folk; on the burghers' narrowness of vision and the decline of federations, and on the struggle for power between kings and feudal lords, when the poor joined royal armies to defeat the hated nobles. The pattern of mutual aid and federalism declined; the "natural" community was supplanted by the artificial state, with kings claiming authority from divine right; and the guilds were replaced by capitalist entrepreneurs. Rather than bemoaning the long decline of mutualism, however, Kropotkin pointed to a modern upsurge of free, voluntary organizations operating outside of state and church control—consumer cooperatives and labor unions—and predicted a time when these institutions would replace the political state as the basis of society.

Nor did Kropotkin hearken back nostalgically to the era of handicrafts as did his friend William Morris, or idealize a pastoral vision as did Tolstoy and, later, Gandhi. Kropotkin was a modernist who wished to harness technology to provide abundance for all. Like the later garden-city theorists such as Lewis Mumford, he foresaw that rapid communications and electric power would equalize small communities and big cities, facilitating a greater rural-urban balance and a reversal of the nineteenth-century trend toward great urban-industrial concentrations.[28] He would have smiled upon the late twentieth-century moves toward "appropriate technology" and the "small is beautiful" school of humanized and downscaled enterprise, and upon the growth of smaller "edge cities" that have mushroomed at the expense of the huge, densely populated cities that date from an earlier era.

As he moved from scientific and historical analysis toward his sociological vision of a just and humanized society, Kropotkin inevitably injected a strong ethical viewpoint into his theorizing. Yet unlike Proudhon, his solutions to contemporary problems were always down-to-earth and not abstract and contradictory; there is a comforting wholeness to his vision. He wanted individuals and their society to regain the balance between city and country, and between intellectual and manual labor, that had been lost with the coming of the industrial revolution and the division of labor. In the tradition of social theorists at least since Thomas More, he condemned overspecialization and sought an integrated approach to education and life.

An integral education would include outdoor activities and direct observation of nature as well as learning through books, combining manual skills with scientific knowledge. An integral city would include garden plots such as those he observed near Paris, where workers could produce their own food. Kropotkin saw evidence all around him of people's desire for a more complete and humanized existence and felt sure that the values he cherished—cooperation rather than competition, harmony rather than destructiveness—would blossom forth if given the chance. Nor did he project a static image of utopia, but rather argued that utopia must be "a living organism continually in development, transforming itself constantly," making possible the "fullest development of individuality combined with the highest development of free association in all its aspects. . . ."[29]

Kropotkin retained the positivist tradition of his predecessors while synthesizing some of the best elements of Proudhon and Bakunin. He accepted much of Proudhon's *ouvrierisme*—or confidence in the workers' ability to manage their own enterprises—and his vision of a decentralized society, and combined it with Bakunin's collectivism and his realization of the need for revolutionary violence to overturn the old order. Where Kropotkin advanced markedly beyond them was in his orientation toward a technological future rather than a romanticized past, all the while retaining the most humane elements from his beloved medieval commune. He also exhibited none of the misogyny and anti-Semitism that marred Proudhon's and Bakunin's thought.

Despite his hopeful, forward-looking philosophy, Kropotkin's last years were not to be happy ones. Even though he had spent time in Clairvaux prison, Kropotkin remained attached to France as the homeland of the great revolution and of the Paris Commune, and so in 1914 he condemned Germany for precipitating the First World War. He felt that if Germany were to win, everything he stood for would be overwhelmed in an orgy of militaristic statism. Most anarchists disapproved of his taking the Allied side, and his position deeply split the movement. For a while the situation brightened, as the February Revolution in Russia in 1917 seemed to confirm all his predictions about the possibility of a spontaneous uprising, with soldiers, workers, and peasants organizing themselves into councils called *soviets* to determine the direction of the revolution. In June 1917 the seventy-five-year-old anarchist returned to his homeland and was offered, and rejected on principle, a position as minister of education and a state pension by Alexander Kerensky. Still, it must have warmed his heart to be greeted by 60 thousand well-wishers and a band playing the *Marseillaise* at Petrograd's Finland Station.[30] The euphoria was not to last.

Soon after the October Revolution, the soviets were reduced to window dressing and all power passed to the Bolshevik party, a fact that Kropotkin decried in a rueful letter to Lenin in March 1920. Within a year Kropotkin was dead. Thousands paraded behind his coffin, and his funeral was the last time the black flag of anarchy was displayed openly in Moscow. In another month—in fact, fifty years to the day that the workers of Paris had proclaimed the Paris Commune—the sailors of the Kronstadt naval base were ruthlessly suppressed by Trotsky in the name of the socialist state. Within a few more months, émigré anarchists Alexander Berkman and Emma Goldman would leave Russia for capitalist but tolerant France, concurring with Kropotkin that bolshevism was the predictable result of authoritarian socialism. The anarchists had the distinction of being the first supporters of the revolution to be locked up.

Gustav Landauer

In the aftermath of the First World War, hopes for social change ran high in many parts of Europe. In the political vacuum created by defeat, revolutionary regimes rose briefly in Germany and Hungary, only to be suppressed by the military or paramilitary forces fearful of the appearance of red revolution. In Berlin in January 1919, the revolutionary socialists Karl Liebknecht and Rosa Luxemburg were murdered by forces loyal to the moderate socialist government; in April, the head of the Bavarian socialist government, the independent socialist Kurt Eisner, was assassinated, and by May the *Freikorps* conquered the city of Munich. Later that summer, the soviet republic of Hungary led by Belâ Kun was crushed, and the danger of revolution from the left receded, only to be replaced by threats on the right.

In Munich, the forces of the state claimed one more notable victim: the anarchist intellectual Gustav Landauer was clubbed to death by troops of the *Reichswehr* and *Freikorps*. Landauer has been called the most important German anarchist thinker since Max Stirner.[31] His thought is difficult to categorize; he called himself an anarchist-socialist, and while he clearly belongs in the anarchist pantheon, his approach to the ideal of a noncoercive society differed considerably from those of his predecessors.

Though Landauer's violent death preceded by two years Kropotkin's peaceful one, he was a generation younger. Born in 1870 in the city of Karlsruhe in southwestern Germany, he came of age in the 1890s at a time when positivism was being challenged throughout Europe. Strongly influenced by the neo-Romantic currents swirling around figures like Schopenhauer, Wagner, Nietzsche, and Ibsen, Landauer brought something new to anarchist thought: Romantic concern for the psyche lying beneath individual consciousness, and a desire to merge oneself with the *volk*, or people. Landauer was a Jewish intellectual who blended anarchist individualism with *völkisch* concern for community and rootedness. This presented two major paradoxes. First, the revolt against positivism was strong throughout Europe, yet it was a German rather than a Spaniard or Frenchman who effected this particular fusion. German anarchists were numerically weak and preponderantly middle-class and Jewish, and thus they lacked the bias against middle-class intellectuals that pervaded the movement elsewhere. Second, in Germany, *völkisch* and irrationalist thought has always been identified with the political right, while the left has been positivist and internationalist. Landauer was no nationalist, yet he and other leftist intellectuals of the turn of the century bore witness that the right had no monopoly on this new intellectual strain, despite the later triumph of fascism.

In some ways, the peculiar conjunction of themes in Landauer's thought should come as no surprise when one is familiar with the heritage of anarchist ideas. Kropotkin was just as concerned with the "natural" community replacing the "artificial" state. What Landauer did was replace Kropotkin's scientific scaffolding with a Romantic interpretation. Rather than seeing the German people reaching fulfillment in the new Reich, he saw the folk community as diverging radically from the centralized state. The individual and the community were overwhelmed by industrialization, mass society, capitalism, and state power, he believed, and must revolt against all these external forces to recapture their original wholeness. Like so many Romantics of the era, he contrasted the soulless *Gesellschaft*, or society, with the rich spirit of *Gemeinschaft*, or community. But the way to utopia did not lie simply in revolution, for the state was not, to Landauer, an institution that could be overturned. Rather, anarchism and statism were both attitudes—were alternative kinds of relationships—and the shift from one to the other required a personal and moral regeneration, not a revolution. One had to change the person before changing the society or attacking the polity. In Landauer's often-quoted words, "The state is a condition, a certain relationship between human beings, a mode of human behavior; we destroy it by contracting other relationships, by behaving differently."[32] Such a spiritual change could not be instituted by terrorist violence or by the general strike, the most common anarchist techniques of the time.

Landauer thus longed for a rebirth of *volk*, community, and humanity. Like Kropotkin, he found the model for this spirit in the medieval commune, but because Landauer was comfortable with religious tendencies alien to Kropotkin's positivist temperament, his medievalism was much more thoroughgoing. He admired medieval society for its spiritual unity. Not this or that *form* of social life—communes, guilds, churches—but "the totality of independent units which all interpenetrate" to form "a society of societies" gave medieval life its beauty.[33] This higher, organic unity of the individual and the community was destroyed by the social atomization and statism of the era of the Reformation. Landauer particularly attacked Luther, no friend of anarchists, for acceding to social and political authority while dissolving medieval social bonds. Yet this new Reformation ethos created its own dialectical spirit; *Geist* was forced underground, but the desire for a true folk community remained. Landauer further diverged from the dialectical materialists in his anti-urban bias, and generally he resembled Proudhon and Bakunin more than Kropotkin in his idealizing of peasants and artisans. Landauer's left-*völkisch* thought reveals an authentic antimodernist streak in anarchism.

With the figures of Landauer and his disciple, the philosopher Martin Buber, we arrive again at utopia. These Jewish intellectuals were not highly influential in their own times. Landauer did play a brief but important role in the Bavarian revolution of 1918–19, and he tried to substitute councils for parliamentary politics in the short-lived *Räterepublik*. For a week he was even minister of education in the radical regime, which was appropriate for someone who believed that the young must be reeducated, to be ready for a libertarian society. Buber was an influential figure in socialist Zionism, and lived to claim the kibbutz movement as the closest approximation of the anarchist ideal. Yet the history of Germany after Landauer's martyrdom was not a happy one for libertarian ideals, and modern Israel shows how Zionism became far more nationalist than anarchist-socialist. These two compelling and tragic figures symbolize the violent collision of anarchist ideals with twentieth-century reality.

3

The Anarchist Movement

Establishing a clear link between theory and practice is even more difficult with anarchism than with socialism. Given anarchists' innate distrust of leaders and centralized organization, there was no way of imposing any sort of theoretical control over the movement. Anarchism produced no theoretician quite comparable to Karl Marx, not because its leaders were intellectually deficient, but because no thinker succeeded as Marx did in demonstrating what appeared to be a superior grasp of historical reality. Nor was there any Karl Kautsky among them to define anarchist "orthodoxy." Anyone who considered government to be fundamentally coercive and thus inimical to one's naturally endowed liberty was an anarchist. Further, many anarchists suspected theorists as being middle-class intellectuals divorced from the experience of the working class. Unfortunately, this combination of theoretical naïveté and distrust of organization hindered the anarchists from adequately describing the process of transition from the present society to that of the future. Not only did ideological purity sometimes lead to ineffectuality, but also anarchists were split among advocates of individualist, mutualist, communist, and syndicalist approaches. Freedom had its costs as well as its benefits.

The divorce of theory from practice did not simply distinguish Russian princes from Parisian café waiters or Spanish peasants. Even more fundamentally, it was the disjunction between ideas and life itself. Notwithstanding all the sophisticated theorizing of a host of anarchist thinkers, anarchism was more an attitude toward power, a way of conducting one's daily life, than it was an application of theory (in fact this was precisely the point Gustav Landauer tried to make—anarchism was the ideal venue for *Lebensphilosophie,* or philosophy of life). One lived an anarchist life rather than practicing anarchist politics, or rather one perceived that relations of power pervaded daily life. An anarchist sought freedom from domination and the right to determine his or her own destiny in workplace, family, and school, while rejecting all forms of hierarchy—that of the academy, of the church, of social class, of "correct" speech as defined by the elites—as well as of those coercive arms of the state, the army, the police, and the judiciary. One did not reject life in order to devote oneself body and soul to the revolution, as Nechaev, Lenin, and all revolutionary puritans from Robespierre onward had maintained; one lived the revolution.

Primitive Rebels

In rejecting political for social revolution, anarchists embraced a total critique of contemporary society, not just the polity. They also tended to imagine the revolution that would usher in the era of anarchy in total terms as a sudden, radical (and perhaps violent) break with the present. Imagery of a night of chaos followed by the new dawn was popular at the end of the century, with a liberated and harmonious society rising out of the ashes. Many commentators have noticed the religious character of the anarchists' desire for a renewed and purified society and have seen it as a modern-day millenarian movement, a throwback to the Anabaptists or Thomas Münzer and the Peasants' Revolt of the Reformation. Millenarian movements are born out of desperation in times of social and moral chaos, arouse great hopes among the populace, and are generally crushed with equally great ferocity. The analysis of anarchism as just such a primitive and ineffectual movement has particularly appealed to Marxists, since it enables them to dismiss it as an irrational throwback, the furthest thing from scientific socialism. If one can tarnish some rivals as utopians, how much more condemnatory are such terms as chiliastic and millenarian.

The millenarian hypothesis further separates anarchist thinkers from the rank and file, for what could a rational positivist such as Proudhon or Kropotkin have in common with an inspired follower seeking not justice or freedom but paradise? There is some truth to the generalization that anarchism functioned like a surrogate religion, but then that point has frequently been made of Marxism (and nationalism too, for that matter). That anarchism functioned as a total belief system, pervading all aspects of life, does not imply that all anarchists were irrational seekers of the absolute. It does suggest that, as with most social movements, it is not enough to consider the ideas of the leadership to understand the real appeal of the movement as a whole.

How, then, did this movement take on a mass character and influence thousands of people in its heyday, between 1880 and 1914? Lacking the formal organization of political parties, how did anarchists spread their ideas, join together, and hope to change society? How did anarchists embody libertarian values in their daily lives? How central was violence to the movement? How did the movement evolve from the days of Proudhon and Bakunin to those of the anarcho-syndicalists on the eve of World War I? As one considers some of the key issues faced by anarchists a century ago, one must remember that they really believed that they were paving the way for a better and radically different society. Anarchism for them was real, not simply an idea.

Organizing Anarchists

Anarchists were notoriously difficult to organize. Anarchists always idealized the federation of autonomous groups who made joint decisions on a voluntary basis. There were occasional congresses of influential anarchists who debated policy and issued nonbinding resolutions. At a congress in 1881, held in London, anarchists voted in favor of propaganda by the deed, which helped set in motion two decades of individual terrorism. In 1889 the anarchists tried to participate in the founding of the Second Socialist International, but memories of the Marx-Bakunin feud that had shattered the First International were still strong, and they were not made to feel welcome. After being expelled from the socialists' Congress of Zurich in 1893, they made a final attempt to be seated at the congress in London in 1896, where Malatesta, Kropotkin, Domela Nieuwenhuis, and Landauer claimed that they, too, were socialists. If parliamentary socialists were seated, they argued, why not antiparliamentary ones? After they were ejected from that meeting, they formed their own congress and never again sought admission with the socialists. At the anarchist assembly, Landauer spoke in favor of the progressive role of the peasantry in shaping cooperative enterprises, which of course would not have been a popular viewpoint among the socialists.[1] Landauer shifted toward anarchism in part out of dislike for the organizational hierarchy of the German Social Democratic Party.

A decade later, the key issue was not the role of peasants but rather that of industrial workers. An international congress was called by Dutch and Belgian anarchists in 1907 in Amsterdam to debate the relative merits of individualist versus syndicalist approaches. The influential Italian anarchist Errico Malatesta remained loyal to the old doctrine of insurrection, while Pierre Monatte of France argued that syndicalism, with its doctrine of the revolutionary general strike, had returned anarchism to its working-class origins and made it possible to link anarchist ideals with reality in direct industrial action.[2] In the decade before World War I the syndicalist approach would hold sway, as anarchists enrolled hundreds of thousands of workers in trade unions.

While socialist workers lined up behind the candidates of the socialist parties, the syndicalists were avid abstentionists, believing that any political participation would co-opt their revolutionary determination. At the French syndicalist congress at Amiens in 1906, the delegates voted to keep their union, the Confédération Général du Travail (CGT), free of all political influence and reaffirmed their revolutionary goals. In the following years they never abandoned their revolutionary rhetoric and even attempted to call some general strikes, but in practice, after 1910, they seemed increasingly to focus on short-term gains, which they argued helped prepare the workers for the coming struggle while improving their economic position. As long as the workers were acting directly on their own behalf, they said, they were gaining valuable experience in organization and confrontation. Anarchist unions remained smaller and much less well funded than socialist unions, making it hard to sustain long strikes, but they made a virtue out of necessity by favoring audacity and activism over mass, bureaucratized institutions.[3] Still, the history of the French CGT bears out Malatesta's fears that unions tended toward reformism, and his belief that a smaller number of pure anarchists was more revolutionary than huge cohorts of lukewarm union members.

After the war, the anarchists attempted to form their own international organization distinct from the Third Communist International, or Comintern, which was run from Moscow. They met between Christmas and New Year's at the end of 1922 in Berlin, dubbed their organization the International Workingmen's Association, and conceived of it as an alliance of labor unions rather than of political parties. This organization did help end the isolation of such national entities as the Spanish syndicalist union, the Confederación Nacional de Trabajo (CNT), but elsewhere anarcho-syndicalism was already in decline and vigorously opposed by communists and capitalists alike. By this time the American syndicalist union, the Industrial Workers of the World (IWW), was already a thing of the past, having suffered severe repression during and after the war. Except in Spain, the heyday of anarcho-syndicalism was over.

Unions were an important way in which the anarchists seriously addressed their organizational deficiencies. The general strike was their new version of a nonpolitical revolution: If the anarchists could organize a large proportion of the workers and indoctrinate them with anarchist ideas, one day they would all lay down their tools, take over the factories, shut down the economy, and watch the state collapse around them. Political revolutions only installed new regimes in power; the general strike would take place on the workers' own terrain. The German socialists condemned revolutionary syndicalism as "general nonsense," and most German workers were enrolled in socialist-led unions, but in France the anarchist CGT numbered 600,000 by 1912; the Spanish CNT had over a million members after the war. Syndicalism found its most famous theorist in a retired French engineer, Georges Sorel. In *Reflections on Violence* (1906), Sorel idealized the general strike as an irrational force employing salutary violence against the force of the state. Inspired by the French philosopher Henri Bergson and turn-of-the-century vitalism, Sorel apotheosized the general strike as a myth designed to motivate and heroize the masses and revive a moribund society. For Sorel, the goals of anarchism were irrelevant; what counted was the experience of the strike itself. As one might expect, his intellectual flights of fancy had minimal impact on the syndicalist rank and file. Sorel influenced Mussolini and other like-minded proponents of action for action's sake more than he ever did anarchism. Most anarchists remained rationalists.

The Era of "Propaganda by the Deed"

The example of Sorel does indicate the appeal of violence, which was strongly associated with anarchism, but the revolutionary strike as a principal means of action was employed only after 1900, following the even more notorious era of individualist violence. Anarchism has long been linked in the popular imagination with terrorism, and the question of the relation between anarchism and terrorism is a difficult and important one. Was the "era of *attentats*," as the French referred to the wave of dynamitings, integral to the anarchist movement—a true reflection of anarchist individualism and negation? Or was it an aberration, a wave of violence perpetrated by lone desperate men largely out of touch with the movement as a whole, venting their personal frustrations against society in the name of anarchism? The answer, as usual, lies somewhere in between, but one can say that anarchism is not reducible to terrorism nor does it necessarily imply violence. For every attention-getting deed there were dozens of anarchist schools, cafés, and cabarets, libraries and theater groups. Anarchists envisioned not chaos but rather a higher kind of order, yet the movement as a whole was stamped as destructive because of the deeds of a relative handful. It would also be incorrect to overidealize the anarchists in the image of Landauer or Tolstoy. As revolutionaries, they were interested in bringing down the old world, some through the example of their own saintly behavior, but others through an apocalypse of smoke and blood. Anarchism resists easy generalizations.

What is now called terrorism was, in the 1870s, called *propaganda by the deed* by the anarchists and referred not to individual but to mass insurrectionary violence. Thus Paul Brousse argued in 1873 that two months of the Paris Commune had done more to propagate the federalist idea than had all the books of Proudhon. Errico Malatesta also used the term as early as 1876, and tried to put it into practice the following year when he encouraged an abortive uprising in Benevento, Italy. Bakunin, too, in the 1870s valued the propaganda value of an insurrectionary act. If such an act would not actually provoke a revolution, at least it would gain more sympathizers.[4] Then came the successful assassination of Czar Alexander II in 1881, which catalyzed the anarchist Congress of London into sanctioning propaganda by the deed. Anarchists did not limit the idea to terrorist acts such as assassinations, however, nor had the members of Narodnaya Volya—the group responsible for the assassination—been anarchists. Kropotkin was less enthusiastic than Malatesta about approving propaganda by the deed, and by the time the wave of violence crested in the 1890s he was disavowing it as an effective revolutionary tool. When the French anarchist-publicist Émile Pouget escaped to England in 1894 to flee the repression that followed the wave of terrorist acts in France, he discovered that most influential anarchists preferred more constructive activity, such as syndicalist organization. When he returned to France the next year he began to promote this new approach in a new edition of *Le Père Peinard,* and eventually came to edit the major organ of syndicalism, *La Voix du Peuple.*

Police suspicions notwithstanding, there was no great anarchist conspiracy to kill heads of state and destabilize governments. Instead, lone men were most often responsible, as they sought to avenge the death or imprisonment of their fellows. The notorious terrorist François Ravachol planted bombs in the homes of a judge and prosecutor in 1892 as retribution for the harsh sentences meted out to May Day protestors the previous year. In June 1894, a young Italian émigré stabbed the president of France, Sadi Carnot, to avenge the executions of earlier anarchist assailants. Italians, in fact, were responsible for the lion's share of the assassinations of heads of state: Premier Cánovas del Castillo of Spain in 1897, Empress Elizabeth of Austria in 1898, and King Umberto of Italy in 1900. Umberto's assailant, Gaetano Bresci, traveled all the way from Paterson, New Jersey, to accomplish his deed. The era of anarchist terrorism coincided with the great wave of Italian emigration, which had no counterpart among Frenchmen or Spaniards. A large pool of poor, displaced, often single young Italian men was thus available, who seemed willing to sacrifice themselves for an ideal and whose fervor was at least in part a result of displaced Catholicism. In 1901, President McKinley of the United States was also assassinated, though by a Pole rather than an Italian. An international antianarchist conference had been convened in Rome in 1898, but it had accomplished little. Harsh laws were passed in Italy, Spain, and France to limit the dissemination of information glorifying violence and to define more broadly what constituted a conspiracy, many anarchist newspapers were closed down and anarchists jailed. Such repression availed little, however, against spontaneous, individual acts.

The irony of this wave of terror so closely associated with

anarchism was that the anarchists had not initiated this sort of terror, nor did their leadership support it. The movement's very theoretical incoherence, its inability to specify how one might achieve anarchist goals, was the underlying cause of the era of propaganda by the deed. Simple souls confused the assassination of a head of state with revolution, or hoped by their example to spur others into action. They conflated the symbolic value of the deed with its instrumental role as catalyst of social revolution. The anarchist leadership perceived this by the 1890s and sought more effective means of action, all the while being reluctant to criticize the bravery and martyrdom of others. The act that aroused almost universal horror was Émile Henry's bombing of a Parisian café in 1894, which he justified cold-bloodedly at his trial by saying, "There are no innocent bourgeois." Henry was unusual in that he was an intellectual terrorist. Only twenty-one years old and the son of a Communard, he had qualified to enter the elite École Polytechnique but had dropped out to pursue his revolutionary career. Most anarchist assailants came from the subproletariat, in striking contrast to the nihilists and populists in Russia, who were mostly well educated and privileged. The Russian intelligentsia saw terror as a quicker alternative to mass revolution,[5] while the Western anarchists mostly sought vengeance for fallen comrades.

The Culture of Anarchism

Propaganda by the deed was only the noisiest of many kinds of propaganda employed by the anarchists in the individualist or "heroic" age of anarchism at the end of the nineteenth century. Anarchists were famous proselytizers, spreading the word by all possible means: by words, songs, and the personal example of a superior life, as well as by deeds. Lacking a firmer sense of how to bring about social revolution, however, they engaged in largely symbolic action. Similarly, anarchist culture was a substitute for formal organization. Anarchists expressed their solidarity at a grassroots level, in the cafés and union halls, in anarchist libraries and schools, and through the anarchist press. In fact anarchists were sometimes suspected of being more involved in living the revolution than in making one. Some were vegetarians and naturopathists, others were nudists or enthusiasts for the international language Esperanto.

Anarchists exulted in the language of the people, seeing in the argot of the lower classes an expression of popular culture remote from the formality of the academies and upper classes. Thus the important French anarchist paper of the 1890s *Le Père Peinard* was written entirely in the slang of the Parisian lower classes. Its editor, Emile Pouget, perceived that this traditional oral culture conveyed its own heritage of illegality and contempt for authority, which he was all too willing to adapt to the anarchist cause. For instance, he used the popular term for pimp, *maquereau* (mackerel), for the members of the Chamber of Deputies, and the legislature was christened the Aquarium. The masthead of the paper featured the image of a cobbler, a typical anarchist calling, and the name of the paper was itself slang for someone who took it easy, expressing the jaundiced anarchist attitude toward work.[6] The anarchists used lower-class argot to reemphasize class divisions and to identify with the subproletariat of bums, thieves, pimps, and prostitutes at the margins of society, as well as the workers.

One other marginal social group that was strongly attracted to anarchism in the late nineteenth century was the bohemians. Artists and would-be artists, poets, singers, and all their hangers-on who inhabited the floating world of art and dreams were captivated by the libertarian ideal of life unconstrained by social conventions. Most were *déclassés* who had rejected their bourgeois parents' values or youths rebelling against parental expectations of a career. Artists who were themselves locked in combat with traditional notions of art felt an immediate kinship with anarchist notions of individuality. Thus a great many modernist artists, from the Impressionists to the Post- and Neo-Impressionists, Fauves, and Cubists, were anarchists. Some, like Camille Pissarro, Maximilien Luce, and Alexandre Steinlen, contributed illustrations to anarchist publications, and money (when they had it) to the cause. Most, as those members of the Parisian artists' colony of Montmartre after the turn of the century, including Pablo Picasso, Kees van Dongen, Maurice Vlaminck, and André Derain,[7] simply felt an affinity for anarchist values.

The relationship between politics and art is always problematic and is especially likely to be contentious when political radicals demand that true revolutionary artists must serve the masses. Should artists strive to make their art popular and intelligible, or should they zealously defend their artistic integrity even at the cost of intelligibility? Proudhon and Kropotkin went out of their way to call artists to serve the revolution, but both had in mind a realist approach that conflicted with the new trends of late-nineteenth-century art.

Anarchists were generally more willing than socialists were to respect artists' freedom to express their revolt against society in their own way. Aesthetic autonomy was even more necessary for the Symbolist poets than for the Post-Impressionist painters, since their esoteric work was unlikely to appeal to working-class anarchists. Poets as distinguished as Stéphane Mallarmé compared their poems to bombs and saw their work as creating an alternative world parallel to the anarchist utopia. Many other writers contributed articles extolling anarchism to literary journals, and the critic Félix Fénéon wrote in colorful slang about the posters of Henri de Toulouse-Lautrec for Le Père Peinard, advising the readers to "liberate" this street art from the walls and kiosks where it was hung. Even that ultimate aesthete, Oscar Wilde, wrote an entire book, slightly misnamed *The Soul of Man Under Socialism*, that dramatized the anarchic qualities of art: "Art is Individualism, and Individualism is a disturbing and disintegrating force. Therein lies its immense value. For what it seeks to disturb is the monotony of type, slavery of custom, tyranny of habit, and the reduction of man to the level of a machine. . . ."[8] Maurice Barrès, later famous for his right-wing nationalism, wrote a book in 1892 called *Enemy of the Laws* that was imbued with the tone of anarchist rebellion, though the anarchist editor Jean Grave opined that this dilettante anarchism was mostly suitable for millionaires. That was partly the point: fin de siècle anarchism appealed to some of the elite as well as to the working class. This was the era in which the ideas of Friedrich Nietzsche captured the interest of the Post-Impressionist and Symbolist generation. The philosopher's persona merged with that of his character Zarathustra, as a hero standing above the conventional morality of the herd. Nietzschean artists felt delivered from empty aestheticism and nihilism; anarchist activism helped restore the vital connection to life preached by the master.

Anarchy ascended to the stage as well. At an 1893 performance in Paris of Henrik Ibsen's play *Enemy of the People*, a young member of the audience described the event in charged terms: "What dynamism and what dynamite! What bombs did we not intend to explode, charged with new explosives, new art . . . bombs that would be fireworks, bouquets of light." Between the scenes, the young radicals "had to defend the cause of Ibsen, of Liberty, of [director] Lugné-Pöe, of the Individual, of Spirit, of Revolt, in the rooms and in the corridors."[9] Three years later, Alfred Jarry's *Ubu Roi* caused an even greater sensation, being compared to an anarchist *attentat* on the audience. Both in their art and in their unconventional daily lives, the fin de siècle artists embodied the anarchist ideal of free creativity.

Sexuality and Gender Roles

Playwright Alfred Jarry's outrageously bohemian life-style, his strange staccato speech, and the loaded pistol he frequently brandished seemed to typify anarchistic rebellion against conventions. One might assume that most anarchists shared such insouciance toward the Emily Posts as well as the Sadi Carnots and William Gladstones of this world, and indeed they did condemn conventional morality as hypocritical. Anarchists pointed frequently to the vast numbers of prostitutes inhabiting European cities as a sign of the rottenness of bourgeois society. Prostitutes played an important symbolic role, standing for the double exploitation of class and sex, and anarchist propaganda portrayed upper-class men preying upon the daughters of the working class. Anarchists' alternatives to social conventions took two very different routes. Some delighted in flouting Victorian norms and pursued paths to sexual freedom while others adopted a strict and conservative code of behavior.

The phrase "free love," *amour libre*, was already current in the 1890s, though it did not refer to promiscuity so much as to the freedom to commence and break off relationships when both partners deemed it in their mutual interest. In England, anarchists were involved in the short-lived journal *The Adult*, which advanced modern ideas concerning sexuality, including homosexuality, until the magazine was suppressed by the authorities. Meanwhile, many anarchist workers and peasants prescribed a more exacting moral code for themselves than that which obtained in the decadent cities of contemporary Europe. Especially in Spain, one found peasants who refused to smoke, drink, or gamble, and who would not consort with prostitutes nor even attend bullfights. These intensely puritanical anarchists hoped to spread their beliefs by their own exemplary behavior, which frequently contrasted with the corrupt morals of the clergy in a way that was reminiscent of the "perfect ones" of the Albigensian heretics in the middle ages. Like the medieval heretics, anarchists were sustained by a moral fervor that transcended rational belief. They wished to purify as well as to transform existing society.[10]

As revolutionaries who believed in altering personal relations, one might expect the anarchists to have held advanced feminist views, but this issue, too, is more complicated than it would at first appear. The European left was no freer of nineteenth-century misogynist attitudes than the right. To combat their sense of themselves as being dominated by the bourgeoisie, left-wing propagandists typically portrayed workers in masculine and virile terms, the symbolic opposite of the prostitute who represented submission. Such portrayals reflected the feelings of manliness and independence workers had when they could provide for their wives and families and shelter them from the vile world of the workplace. The right to vote was not highly valued among anarchists, but it is worth noting in this context that among the socialists who pursued electoral politics, many opposed female suffrage because they feared that women in Catholic Europe were more conservative than men and that they would be particularly influenced by their priests. Male workers also feared that women would displace them in the factories because employers could pay them lower wages. This led French syndicalists to support equal pay for women, not out of support for feminist equality but because they reasoned that with equal pay employers would prefer male workers and the women would return home. At the same time, they argued that capitalism denatured the working-class home, that factories endangered pregnant women, and that, consequently, women should be protected from exploitation.[11]

These anarcho-syndicalists also cited Proudhon to justify their arguments. Proudhon has frequently been called a misogynist for his traditional and puritanical ideas concerning women's roles and sexuality. He lashed out at the sexual libertinism of the followers of Saint-Simon, disliked "the high-toned lady, the female artist or writer," and strongly believed that a woman's place was in the family. In *Pornocraty, or Women in Modern Times* he condemned the loose morality of the Second Empire and argued instead for monogamous marriage. His moralistic alternatives for women were the roles of housewife or harlot. Much of this prejudice was due to his reverence for the family as the fount of morality and sobriety. He feared the incursions of the modern world on family life, and so just as he defended peasant and artisanal values, he also wished to keep the wife at home. Yet he went beyond merely wishing to preserve family life. In his 1858 book, *Justice in the Revolution and the Church,* he insisted that women were both physically and intellectually inferior to men, though he acknowledged them to be superior in beauty, intuition, and the capacity for love.[12]

The other male anarchist thinkers were surprisingly unconcerned about women's role in society. Even the wide-ranging Kropotkin had little to say on the issue and inadvertently revealed sexist attitudes in his appeal to artists: "fire the hearts of our youth with that glorious revolutionary enthusiasm which inflamed the souls of our ancestors. Tell women what a noble career is that of a husband who devotes his life to the great cause of social emancipation."[13] Kropotkin's emphasis on the objective forces leading the world toward anarchy led him to minimize the role of personal relations. In some ways he was too much the scientist and benign sage to fully appreciate the emotional appeal of the anarchist call for personal liberation. Such striking omissions by the great theorists of anarchism are all the more disturbing when contrasted with the serious work being done by the socialists of the same era: Auguste Bebel's *Woman Under Socialism* (1883) and Friedrich Engel's *The Origin of the Family, Private Property and the State* (1884).

Anarchism nevertheless attracted some outstanding women. Louise Michel of France, the "red virgin of the Commune"; Americans Emma Goldman, Voltairine de Cleyre, and Mollie Steimer; England's Charlotte Wilson, who was a catalyst in establishing an anarchist movement in that country; and Federica Montseny of Spain were only the most prominent. A Chinese anarchist, a woman named He Zhin who lived in Japan, argued in the early twentieth century that women must be liberated from the three "followings"— father, husband, and son—and condemned Chinese practices of foot binding, polygamy, and filial piety. In such a repressive context feminism was undeniably revolutionary.[14]

Anarchist feminists did not join the mainstream of the nineteenth-century women's movement in upholding the purity of women as nurturers and guardians of morality, nor were they eager to attain the right to vote. They denied the existence of sex-based intellectual or psychological differences, unequivocally demanded economic independence as the prerequisite of individuality, and frankly avowed female sexuality. Their own sexual lives were often unconventional. Their radical positions, which challenged the cult of domesticity and the family, sometimes brought them into conflict with their male counterparts.[15]

Feminist socialists have always had to contend with the argument that the revolution must precede equality between the sexes. The party line has generally been that with the elimination of bourgeois capitalism will come the end of exploitive social relations, including those of men over women. Even the most casual glance at the Soviet Union renders this theory suspect. The anarchists presented a cogent critique of "revolutionary deferral" in gender relations as in other areas—but it took an outstanding female anarchist to enunciate this position.

Federica Montseny was to anarchy born, the daughter of anarchist intellectuals who published both a newspaper and journal in which Montseny could air her views. Born in 1905, by the 1920s she was already publishing novels as well as articles dramatizing the plight of Spanish women, and arguing that a libertarian society could not be established until a revolution occurred between the sexes. As were most Spanish anarchists she was strongly anticlerical and antireligious, and she particularly condemned the church's hold over women. The church fostered female ignorance; education was central to her vision of emancipated womenhood, not least because only educated women could raise children freed from bondage to tradition and the church. So without a radical change in women's status, the anarchists' dreams of a better future would remain dreams. Montseny advocated free union between individuals based on natural morality, which would give rise to spontaneous love between equals. Love implied freedom, the perfect balance of reason and passion, while marriage killed love and stifled women's freedom. She warned women of the 1920s not to masculinize themselves by wearing pants and short hair, but rather to aspire to be a woman and a human being.[16]

Montseny later became the only woman ever to hold a ministerial portfolio in a Spanish government—an ironic distinction for an anarchist. The times, however, were not ordinary, as she joined the coalition popular front government during the Spanish civil war, becoming minister of health and public assistance for a short time before the communists forced the anarchists from all positions of power. Meanwhile, in the unions and collectives dominated by the anarcho-syndicalist CNT, the women did the homemaking, baking, and washing. A Mujeres Libres (Free Women) column was even organized so women could wash and iron at the front![17] Montseny was surely right in demanding that feminism precede the revolution.

A necessary adjunct to feminism was birth control, which some anarchists saw as a form of direct action—"bellies on strike," as they put it. Aside from the issue of women having control over their bodies, it was argued that too many children created unemployment and depressed wages, and that having fewer children would allow workers more time to concentrate on the class struggle, which was undoubtedly true. Paul Robin was one early neo-Malthusian or supporter of birth control, publishing a journal called *Regeneration*. In 1900 the first international conference of birth-control leagues took place in Paris, and the French syndicalist CGT later gave the policy its unofficial support.[18] In Catholic France, at a time when birth rates were stagnant and there was widespread fear of being outstripped demographically by the Germans, this was a radical stance. In the United States, where the Comstock Act proscribed the spread of family planning information as obscene, the birth-control issue was linked to that of free speech. From the 1870s to the 1890s, New Englander and individualist anarchist Ezra Heywood was repeatedly jailed for mailing articles discussing sexuality and birth control. Emma Goldman spoke out forcefully in its favor in her wide-ranging lecture tours of the country before and during World War I, actively disseminating the birth control pamphlets of Margaret Sanger. She and her manager/lover Ben Reitman were jailed for these activities during the First World War.

Education

The other issue central to Federica Montseny's vision of liberation, education, was an area of abiding interest to many anarchists of both sexes. Kropotkin took a typical anarchist position in arguing for what was commonly called integral education, that is, integrating intellectual and manual labor, book learning balanced by experience of the real world. Proudhon, too, wished to combine industrial and literary instruction, producing "the man of industry, the man of action and the man of intelligence all at once."[19] Being anarchists, Kropotkin and Proudhon also stressed the development rather than the taming of individual talents and proclivities, and the equality of student and teacher. The influential French anarchist Sebastien Faure opened a school 50 kilometers from Paris called The Hive, which he ran from 1904 until the war. His "school of tomorrow" was explicitly opposed to the schools run both by the church and by the state. Between twenty and forty boys and girls lived and studied there, attending class until age twelve, after which they divided their time between their studies and work in the fields and workshops.[20]

Perhaps the most famous practitioner of these ideas was Francisco Ferrer, who was born near Barcelona in 1859 and died there fifty years later, executed in the aftermath of the Tragic Week, as the bloody uprising of 1909 was called. After living for a long time in Paris, where he developed his views on education, Ferrer returned to Barcelona in 1901 to open his Escuela Moderna, or Modern School. Ferrer's chief goal was to provide a rationalist alternative to the Catholic church's stranglehold over Spanish schools, to free his students' minds from "the false concepts of property, country and family" and to develop their rational and critical capacities.[21] He also encouraged the practical rather than the theoretical approach, preferring field trips and experiments to knowledge gained second-hand. Yet Ferrer was not averse to books; in fact he was soon involved in publishing libertarian literature for all ages. Nor did he confine his attentions to educating children; he also ran an adult education center. Libertarian schools attempted to be perfect microcosms of anarchist institutions, conveying ideals of untrammeled creativity and self-development through noncoercive means. As well as embodying anarchist ideals, schools like Ferrer's also served as centers of agitation. Both of these aspects of the Escuela Moderna, the ideal and the propagandistic, incurred the wrath of Spanish authorities in direct proportion to the success of Ferrer's efforts. By 1905, not only were 126 students enrolled there, but there were also already fourteen other libertarian schools in Barcelona and thirty-four more elsewhere in Spain based on his model.[22] Then, in 1906, an anarchist who worked at Ferrer's publishing house was apprehended for having attempted to assassinate King Alfonso XIII. It is unclear whether Ferrer was involved in the assassination plot—he loudly proclaimed his innocence—but the authorities used the occasion as an excuse to close down his school.

Ferrer's martyrdom in 1909 for the cause of free thinking led to protest demonstrations around the world; in Paris, 15,000 people stormed the Spanish Embassy. Emma Goldman played an active role in establishing a Ferrer Association in the United States, and over the next four years anarchist schools opened in cities across the country. Modern Schools based on Ferrer's model were founded throughout Europe and as far afield as Argentina and China over the next thirty years.[23] In the Ferrer School in New York City, a young teacher named Will Durant fell in love with a fourteen-year-old student whom he rechristened Ariel. Their romance hastened his departure from the Ferrer School; she later became his collaborator in their immensely popular history of civilization, a project itself rooted in the anarchist impulse to educate the masses. As with most of the faculty, Durant was a well-educated, native-born American; like most of the students, Ariel came from a family of Eastern European Jewish immigrants. Other students at the school included Amour Liber (amour libre is French for free love), and his cousins Hyperion, Gorky, and Révolte Bercovici. Their parents were Rumanian Jews who had first emigrated to Paris, where they attended the Université Populaire in the working-class Faubourg St. Antoine, before going to New York.[24]

The Ferrer School of New York was much more than a place to educate young people along anarchist principles of rational self-development. Located near Harlem just a few blocks from the editorial office of Emma Goldman's journal, *Mother Earth*, it served in the evening as a cultural center attracting a brilliant bohemian crowd, including Sadakichi Hartmann, Hippolyte Havel, Alexander Berkman, and Man Ray, among many others. In March 1914 the Ferrer Center hosted a symposium on the Paris Commune; two months later it commemorated the centennial of the birth of Mikhail Bakunin with speeches by Berkman and Havel and music by the Modern School Trio. Feminists such as Margaret Sanger and Elizabeth Gurley Flynn (the "rebel girl") spoke there, not as proponents of women's suffrage but rather on birth control and women in the labor movement. In 1914 a theater company found a home at the school, and well-known artists such as Robert Henri and George Bellows conducted art classes there. At their best, these schools greatly enhanced the vibrant anarchist cultural milieu on the eve of the First World War. The Modern School Association of North America was disbanded in the late 1950s, just before the British educator A. S. Neill's book *Summerhill: A Radical Approach to Child-Rearing* rekindled interest in libertarian educational ideals. In the 1960s, free schools sprang up once again across the United States; some, like the Walden School in Berkeley, California, were established by Modern School alumni.[25]

Anarchists as well as socialists were eager to provide educational opportunities for workers in the evenings, organizing "popular universities" to broaden their horizons. When these ventures were supported by the government, as they were in France between 1896 and 1914, their curriculum tended to broaden beyond purely anarchist issues. These, too, were centers of popular entertainment in the evenings, providing an alternative to the saloon in working-class neighborhoods.

Anarchists were also tempted to leave the dominant society behind and create their own "free milieus." Some organized cooperatives in the cities, others rented or bought land in the country to farm communally. Country living demanded a wide array of skills, encouraging a sense of self-sufficiency, while also tapping into anarchist ideals of living in harmony with nature. The New York Ferrer School left the city after a series of bombs promised to tarnish the school with suspicions of terrorism. After some debate about the school's responsibility to its tenement-bound constituency, it was moved in 1915 to Stelton, New Jersey, near New Brunswick, and there pursued more aggressively the experiential approach to education while downgrading bookish knowledge. The Stelton school reached a peak of success in the 1920s and lasted until the 1950s. Learning, not farming, was central to the community of Stelton, and many residents commuted into New York for jobs. Propelled more by an intense desire for autonomy than by practical experience with farming, most rural anarchists did not succeed in their communal efforts.

One can multiply endlessly the variety of approaches to the anarchist vision of a liberated society, but all were born of the desire to embody the principles of the revolution rather than either theorizing or endlessly plotting one. In this sense anarchists were practical revolutionaries, not chiliasts awaiting the judgment day. On the other hand, their intense desire to "live the revolution" dispersed their energies and, arguably, made it less likely that the revolution would ever come.

World War I and the Russian Revolution

One of the most striking aspects of the anarchist movement was the rapidity of its decline. On the eve of World War I it represented a viable alternative to the socialist model of change, although the syndicalist unions were dwarfed in size by the socialist ones, and the anarchists had nothing to compare, of course, to the numerous socialist deputies being elected to national legislatures by millions of working-class voters. Precisely because socialism had lost its revolutionary edge, there was room on the left for anarchism and anarcho-syndicalism, with their vision of imminent and fundamental change. Then came the war, which demonstrated the depth of nationalist fervor, and the Bolshevik Revolution, which reclaimed the socialist vision of revolution while exemplifying just how such a revolution could be made. After 1920, anarchism as a mass revolutionary movement remained alive only in Spain and parts of Latin America, which had remained neutral during World War I. The combination of communism and fascism in the emerging totalitarian temper of the 1930s would root out this last great bastion of libertarian enthusiasm. In Russia and Spain, however, the anarchists did not surrender without a fight.

The failure of the workers on the left to unite in opposing the call to arms in 1914 is well known. The German socialists voted the Kaiser his war credits; the French government never needed to activate its list of union leaders and militants who were to be arrested to forestall strikes and protests that might impede general mobilization of the armed forces of France. Were the anarchist leaders cowards or hypocrites, or did they discover that they were Frenchmen first, anarchists second? It has been previously noted that genuine confusion prevailed about what was the correct political attitude to take in the West in the face of a German invasion. June 1914 witnessed "Red Week" in Italy as an anarchist-dominated united front of antimilitarist committees staged massive protests against war. For a while a general strike loomed, but the Italian General Confederation of Labor was not controlled by the anarchists, and when the union leaders called off the strike the revolt collapsed. On the other hand, Peter Kropotkin himself endorsed the French war effort as necessary to stop the greater evil of German militarism. Most anarchists, including Errico Malatesta, who joined Kropotkin in London after the failure of the Italian revolt, did not agree with Kropotkin. Yet by July 1914, the head of the French syndicalist union, Léon Jouhaux, knew that if war came German workers would march, and so a call for a general strike would not lead to an international strike against war. To call for such a strike would have endangered France and destroyed the CGT.

The war itself strengthened the French labor movement, as the government discovered how much it needed labor's cooperation, but it did largely end anarchist influence over the unions. By the end of the war the unions had tacitly accepted state authority, all the while remaining aloof from any one political party. Not until the 1930s did the communist party make serious incursions into the CGT, and when it did so the union was fragmented, as the anarcho-syndicalists broke off to form their own CGTSR, the appended letters standing for "revolutionary syndicalist."[26]

Anarchists had always opposed government in all forms and had reserved a special hatred for the military as the most hierarchical and coercive arm of government. They condemned those socialists who tolerated a measure of cooperation with the bourgeois parliamentary state. Yet by 1917 the chief anarchist theoretician had supported the war effort on one side in the conflict, the anarchists themselves had colluded with the French state, and the socialists of Russia had demonstrated that socialism had retained its revolutionary edge. Lenin, unlike Kropotkin, was unequivocally opposed to the war and attracted great popularity with his promise of immediate land, bread, and peace for the suffering people of Russia. The triumph of communism in Russia thus sowed considerable confusion in anarchist ranks throughout the West until at least 1921. Within Russia itself, anarchists as well as socialists played an active role in the revolutionary turmoil, but that role has been forgotten, and anarchists themselves were suppressed by the communists.[27]

Anarchism in Revolutionary Russia

One would expect the homeland of Bakunin and Kropotkin to have sheltered an indigenous anarchist movement, and yet no such movement existed in the 1860s and 1870s when Bakunin's influence was greatest and Kropotkin was beginning his revolutionary career. The real history of Russian anarchism unfolded between 1903 and 1921. If anarchism appealed to the workers of the less developed regions of Europe, including the peasants of Andalusia, why did it find so few converts in Russia? Anarchism has tended to thrive in societies in transition toward modernity, especially those with strong artisanal traditions, and Russian anarchists did tend to come either from artisanal or intellectual backgrounds. Since Russian socialists remained revolutionary, unlike their Western European counterparts, the anarchists were unable to present themselves as the most viable radical alternative. Most peasants identified with the Social Revolutionary (SR) party, most workers with the Social Democrats (SD), which was Marxist. A disproportionate number of Russian anarchists were Jews from the Pale of Settlement who had experienced intensified persecution from the central government after the assassination of Czar Alexander II. From Bialystok to Warsaw, Vilna,

Minsk, and Riga, they soon spread to Odessa and Kiev in the Ukraine, often among disaffected SRs and SDs.[28] Russian anarchists were thus even more socially marginal than was the norm in the West.

Since anarchism as well as modernity came to Russia later than to Western Europe, most of the ideas and influence flowed from west to east. At the peak of the movement, after the 1905 Revolution, there may have been 5,000 anarchist activists, plus thousands more sympathizers. They were split, however, into several groups that mirrored differing Western influences, and this lessened their effectiveness. The Bakuninists favored revolutionary terror and conspiracy, and after the 1903 socialist split between Bolsheviks and Mensheviks they especially disdained the Marxist doctrine that Russia must pass through a parliamentary and capitalist phase before socialist revolution would be possible. The anarchists exalted fervor and will over class analysis. Kropotkin condemned conspiratorial violence not predicated on the prior mobilization of the masses. His followers, called anarchist-communists, were akin to the populist Slavophiles in their favoring of handicrafts and agricultural communes. Finally, syndicalism was exported directly from France to Russia around 1903, with its doctrine of worker organization and the general strike. Kropotkin generally supported syndicalism but felt that it was too narrowly based to include artisans and peasants; nor did he entirely trust the unions not to seek accommodation with their bourgeois bosses.

The February Revolution was an anarchist's dream come true: a spontaneous movement of soldiers, workers, and peasants who immediately created workers' councils and sought to end the war and expropriate the landlords. Some anarchists returned to Petrograd from New York, where they began fomenting opposition to the provisional government. In the summer of 1917, their only real ally in this opposition to the government was Lenin, and after the premature coup of July failed, he went into hiding. But the anarchists remained both divided among themselves and incapable of dominating the factory councils or the soviets. Instead, Lenin seemed to support syndicalist ideals of worker control, much as he appropriated SR ideals of agrarian reform, and so he outflanked both groups. Lenin went so far as to say, in *State and Revolution*, that the state and freedom were irreconcilable enemies. The anarchists erroneously assumed that he supported the latter option. In 1917, Lenin and the anarchists were allies on the extreme left of the political spectrum;

within three years of Lenins' taking power, he would brutally eliminate them.

Immediately after the October Revolution of 1917, Lenin did authorize direct workers' control of all enterprises employing five or more workers. Factory committees were responsible to local councils of workers, who reported in turn to the All-Russian Council of Workers' Control. The atomization and economic chaos resulting from this system, however, were seemingly intolerable to Lenin. Just as the soviets became democratic window dressing for Communist Party control, so factory committees became unions beholden to the party, and the enterprises came under direct state control.[29]

In March 1918, Lenin ceded to Germany all of western Russia. The anarchists condemned the Treaty of Brest-Litovsk and called for partisan warfare in the spirit of 1812. In April, the Bolshevik secret police, the Cheka, raided twenty-six anarchist centers in Moscow; by May, 40 anarchists were dead, 500 taken prisoner, and the anarchist press shut down.

If the history of Russian anarchism had ended here, it would indeed be no more than a footnote to the triumph of Marxist socialism. Instead, anarchists went on to control a significant portion of Russian territory during the civil war that engulfed the country until 1921. The black flag of anarchy waved over the Ukraine, thanks to the daring exploits of Nestor Makhno (1889–1934), a peasant who arose, like an apparition of the cossack bandit-chieftains Stenka Razin and Emelyan Pugachev, to lead his people of the steppe. Makhno spent the years from 1908 to 1917 in prison for a terrorist attack, which only confirmed for him his early anarchist sympathies. He returned to his native village after the February Revolution, and was soon elected chairman of his local Soviet of Workers' and Peasants' Deputies. He also led the peasants in raids to expropriate the estates of the local gentry, until the Treaty of Brest-Litovsk allowed German and Austrian troops to occupy the area. Makhno fled to Moscow, where in the summer of 1918 he met both Kropotkin and Lenin. He soon returned to the Ukraine to organize partisan raids on the invaders and their local puppets, finding shelter and support among the peasant population. After he defeated a superior force of Austrians and their Ukrainian sympathizers in September 1918, his men conferred upon him the affectionate title of *bat'ko*, or little father. When the First World War ended, he seized some of the Austrians' equipment to wage war on Ukrainian nationalists.[30]

Then came an extraordinary period in which for half a year no political authority controlled the Ukraine, and Makhno was free to set up a libertarian society. Regional Congresses of Peasants, Workers, and Insurgents were held between January and April 1919 to decide how to defend the territory and encourage the election of free soviets in the villages (free, that is, from political party influence). In March 1919, he agreed to joint military action against the White Army of General Denikin, while fighting under the black banner of the Insurgent Army of the Ukraine. Over the next year and a half, Trotsky, as head of the Red Army, accepted his anarchist ally only out of necessity; at each sign of success against the Whites, he immediately tried to dominate or suppress the Makhnovite forces. With the threat of counterrevolution over, he turned on Makhno's commanders in the Crimea and had them shot in November 1920. Trotsky then seized Makhno's headquarters in his home village of Gulyai-Polye. Makhno himself escaped, along with a few of his supporters, and made his way to Rumania and eventually to Paris. He ended his life working in an automobile factory, drinking heavily, dying of tuberculosis at the age of 44.

Like the attempts in Spain to reorganize society along anarchist lines during the fight against Franco in 1936–38, Ukrainian anarchism was a short-lived phenomenon that took place against a backdrop of civil war. Unlike the Spanish case, which, as we will see, was centered in an industrialized city (Barcelona), Makhnovite anarchism was almost entirely a peasant affair, and Makhno himself a pure example of the "primitive rebel." As a peasant schooled in anarchist thought, Makhno readily tapped traditional peasant hatred of the landlords and the state, with its tax collectors and recruiting officers. His primary social accomplishment was to establish agricultural communes based on Kropotkin's principles of mutual aid, with the land and kitchens worked in common. He also attempted to stimulate worker self-management—among railway workers, for instance—but his experiments among wage-dependent workers did not fare well.[31] Though he did preserve discipline in his army, Makhno's commanders were also peasants or, occasionally, shop workers. Wherever his army went, he declared to the peasants that now they were free of all authority, he proclaimed freedom of speech, press, and assembly, and he threw open the prison doors. Makhno pioneered the guerrilla tactics that would be used by future peasant revolutionaries of the Third World.

Much of Makhno's short-lived success depended on his unique personality, yet he did demonstrate for the first time that anarchism was not just a dream of intellectuals or princes; its principles could find resonance among the people. Lenin told Makhno that the problem with anarchists was that they were only capable of envisioning the future, not of acting in the present. Makhno proved Lenin wrong. Opposing both the gentry and the commissars, he was at once a cossack hero of the steppe and an anarchist liberator. Anarchism succeeded best when it framed its appeal in traditional terms and mobilized immediate popular support by means of direct action. The most fertile soil for the fruition of anarchist principles was not to be in the wheat fields of the Ukraine but in the vineyards of Spain.

4

Case Study: Anarchism in Spain

Anarchism spread beyond the confines of Europe to spawn diverse movements in Latin America and the United States, in Australia, even in China and India. In the Old World, it encountered the greatest mass support in Latin Europe, whereas in England and Germany it remained largely a middle-class movement. Nowhere else did anarchism achieve the depth of fervor and the breadth of support that it found in Spain. For seventy years, from the late 1860s until the fascist triumph in the Spanish civil war, on the eve of World War II, anarchism posed a significant threat to the established order. At its peak in the 1930s, the anarcho-syndicalist labor union, the Confederación National de Trabajo (CNT), numbered a million and a half adherents. At one point during the civil war, the popular front government felt it necessary to offer ministerial portfolios to four anarchist leaders—and the anarchists felt it necessary to accept them. Anarchist collectives were set up throughout the Spanish states of Aragon and Catalonia, while anarchist militias fought along the Ebro River. All this occurred after anarchism had declined in influence elsewhere in Europe.

Spain offers the best opportunity to observe anarchism not simply as an ideal or as a motivator of violent deeds, but actually to see it in practice. It raises the possibility of an answer to the question of whether anarchism can work; whether anarchists can build as well as dream and destroy. The Spanish civil war offers the spectacle of anarchists in contention with republicans, fascists, and communists, and reveals their vulnerability to centrally directed and hierarchically organized power.

Cultural Roots

Wherever anarchism has taken hold, it has done so because its values have meshed with those of the local culture. Anarchists have excelled at channeling prepolitical levels of awareness into more modern and theoretical forms. Trying to explain why a movement such as anarchism encounters popular support at a particular place and time requires that one weigh objective and subjective factors. Does the populace respond to such a movement because the ideology is appropriate for a particular level of economic and social development, or because it expresses certain cultural values? For Spain, the answer must be both. Spain in the years between 1868 and 1938 fit the model that has proved especially receptive to anarchist ideas: a backward, and developing society in transition toward capitalism and industrialization. Peasants, day laborers, artisans, and newly urbanized factory workers, as well as artists and intellectuals, all responded to anarchist propaganda. But anarchism did not simply reach Spain at the right time; Spain was uniquely the right place.

Despite the best efforts of the Spanish kings since the time of Ferdinand and Isabella, Spaniards remained generally hostile to centralized government and to the dominance of Madrid and the province of Castile. The other regions—Catalonia, Aragon, Valencia and Murcia, Andalusia, the Basque country—resented Castilian domination. Certainly society was riven by class distinctions, but questions of geography predominated at least until the nineteenth century. Spanish federalism was securely in place long before the ideas of Proudhon spread from across the Pyrenees. The forces for centralization remained relatively weak at the very moment that Spain's European neighbors were coalescing into modern industrial nation-states. Government in Madrid remained divorced from the industrial development going on in Barcelona and Bilbao; prosperity thus reinforced rather than dampened demands for cultural autonomy. At the local level, people were fiercely proud of their independent *pueblos,* a term that referred to the common people and to the village itself, thereby marking the rich as outsiders. Anarchists encountered a people inclined toward self-sufficiency and autonomy, intensely proud and moralistic, used to identifying corrupt practices with the privileged classes, and therefore accepting the egalitarian virtues of poverty.

Yet if Spaniards were often hostile to the state, were they not deeply devout Catholics? The answer is that they had been until the nineteenth century, and many remained devout even as they turned away from the institution of the Catholic church. In the course of the nineteenth century the Church increasingly turned toward the elites—ironically, because the liberal government of the 1830s confiscated the landed property of the church and so made the clergy financially dependent on the wealthy classes. Parish priests remained poor, however, so they began charging fees for their services, which scarcely endeared them to the people. During Holy Week they would march through the villages under a canopy held up by a civil guard and a township official, epitomizing for the people the close relationship between church and state.[1] Far more despised than the parish priests were the monks, about whom the common people enjoyed spreading tales of licentious behavior. The clergy were perceived to be soft idlers who would do better to work for their living. The church also fought a rear-guard action against secular education in a country where the majority of citizens in 1870 were still illiterate. Into the spiritual void created by the increasing alienation of church and people stepped anarchism.[2]

It is tempting to see anarchism as a surrogate religion seized upon by the Spanish people as the road to salvation. Anarchism ultimately promised a spiritual rather than material paradise of austere equality and freedom from domination by political bosses and landlords. Spanish anarchists tended to be puritanical, refraining from alcohol, tobacco, and the brothel as a sign of their moral superiority over the decadent elites. Above all, anarchism promised that the millennium was within reach, that the revolution could break through at any time and abolish instantly the corrupt old order, ushering in the perfect society of anarchy, or natural order. Nowhere has the millenarian explanation for the appeal of anarchism seemed to fit better than in Spain, where in the nineteenth century the *braceros,* the landless laborers of Andalusia, formed the largest contingent of anarchist support. And no one has found this explanation of anarchism's appeal more appealing than the Marxists.

In his influential book *Primitive Rebels*, the British Marxist historian Eric Hobsbawm included the peasant anarchists of Andalusia, along with Italian mafiosi and Robin Hood-style banditi, under the rubric announced by the title. Their rebellion against the authorities, he said, was prepolitical, that is pre-Marxist, informed less by rational ideology than by quasi-religious longing for a better world. Hobsbawm admitted that anarchist ideas of spontaneous direct action fit the peasant's mood perfectly, but that this very identity between ideology and popular sentiment condemned all their efforts to failure, for it "utterly failed to teach them the necessity of organization, strategy, tactics, and patience, it wasted their revolutionary energies almost completely."[3] Anarchism encouraged direct action at the local level, along with millenarian dreams of the *reparto* (distribution) when all the land would be repossessed by the people. In practice, Hobsbawm said, this led to periodic uprisings, uncoordinated on a national basis, that would be brutally crushed, driving the movement underground for a number of years until social frustrations reached another boiling point and the process would recommence.

There is some truth to this criticism, just as there is truth to the broadly cultural approach that sees anarchistic traits residing within the Spanish character. Yet neither explanation is sufficient. Just as there were good socioeconomic reasons for Spaniards to choose anarchism, so it is simplistic to see their adherence as irrational. Granted the Spaniards had a quasi-religious streak, but they also had a rational ideology, legitimate forms of organization such as trade unions, and limited, practical ends in mind, not just vague notions of *reparto*. Nor were all Andalusian anarchists illiterate peasants; many adherents came from the towns, and throughout Spain anarchists increasingly found supporters among the urban working class as well as among intellectuals.[4]

The Bakuninist Origins of Spanish Anarchism

The rise of anarchism in the 1860s coincided with the collapse of the central government in Spain. Queen Isabella lost her throne in 1868 at the very moment that Mikhail Bakunin was forming his Alliance of Social Democracy in Switzerland. Within a month, some prominent French followers of Bakunin visited Barcelona, and shortly thereafter Bakunin's emissary Giuseppe Fanelli made a rapid tour of Spain, meeting with labor leaders and others to spread Bakunin's ideas. Fanelli's inability to speak Spanish notwithstanding, his ideas were received enthusiastically in Barcelona and Madrid. Listeners reported on the dramatic tone of his voice as he described the suffering of the exploited, and the message got across. (This too might be taken as evidence of Spanish anarchism's largely emotional impact.) Spain soon had its own section of the International Working Men's Association, the "International" founded by Marx in 1864 to which the anarchists still belonged. When the anarchists were drummed out of the International a few years later, they remained loyal to Bakunin, and socialism remained weak in Spain right up to the 1930s. In fact Spain provided the issue over which Marx banished Bakunin from the organization, after Marx's son-in-law, Paul Lafargue, traveled to Spain in 1872 and found evidence that Bakunin's Alliance still existed there, despite the Russian revolutionary's claims that he had dissolved it.[5]

However enthusiastic Giuseppe Fanelli must have been, the rapid dissemination of anarchist ideas in Spain owed more to the chaotic political situation and the receptivity of the artisans and professionals with whom he met than to his innate charisma. The anarchists held congresses in Barcelona in 1870—where they set up the Spanish wing of the International amid debates between Proudhonian federalists and Bakuninist collectivists—in Valencia in 1871, and in Córdoba in 1872. In 1871 the revolutionary events of the Paris Commune magnified the importance of the International in the eyes of the Spanish authorities and also spurred its growth. The International's high point of influence came in 1873 during the short-lived Spanish Republic. A federalist and a follower of Proudhon, the Catalan Francisco Pi y Margall, briefly became head of the government in 1873, with the intention of disseminating power to the provinces. Unfortunately for him, Spain dissolved into fighting, and the army stepped in to restore order, soon ending the republican experiment and outlawing the International. For a while in 1873 the Cantonalist movement that encouraged cities in Andalusia such as Málaga, Seville, and Granada, as well as Cartagena, Valencia, and Barcelona on the eastern coast, to set up their own governments seemed to be following the direction of the Paris Commune. As in Paris, anticlericalism asserted itself; the churches of Barcelona were closed for several months, while in Seville they voted to convert the cathedral into a café. In a small town between Valencia and Alicante called Alcoy, fighting broke out between the workers and the police and cost a dozen lives on each side. Yet in all of this the Bakuninists played a relatively small role, and despite the Alcoy uprising failed to provoke a general strike in Barcelona. When they tried to call for one after the army dismissed the Spanish parliament, they were forced underground.

In these insurrectionary early years of Spanish anarchism, the general strike was the favored Bakuninist method of bringing about social revolution while avoiding overtly political action. After Bakunin died and his movement was suppressed, the anarchists began to turn to terrorism, and in 1878 an attempt was made on the life of the new Bourbon king of Spain, Alfonso XII, by a young Catalan member of the International. Some of the anarchists supported direct action in any form; others clung to Bakunin's vision of an elite corps of revolutionaries guiding a mass insurrection of the people when conditions again turned propitious. Still another group of mostly Barcelona anarchists rejected the move toward premature violence and favored instead the syndicalist tactics of organizing the workers into both industrial and agricultural unions, "the living germs of the new social order." This group therefore rejected the clandestine modes favored by the terrorists in favor of a policy designed to regain legal recogition.[6] This debate between the insurrectionists, the terrorists, and the syndicalists would continue into the twentieth century, until it culminated in the founding of the CNT in 1910. By that time Spain would be rapidly industrializing and anarchism would have changed from a mostly peasant to a primarily industrial-worker base. In the meantime Spain would encounter the whole range of anarchist tactics, from the spontaneous peasant uprisings of Jerez to the terrorist bombings of Barcelona.

The 1890s

What seems clear from the Spanish case is that, unlike the Russian nihilists who focused on political assassination as a self-sufficient policy designed to discredit the regime, the Spanish anarchists used terror or propaganda by the deed mostly as a response to government repression and not as an end in itself. Bombs thrown by lone individuals were more difficult to suppress than were mass actions, such as general strikes, and were equally impossible for the anarchists themselves to proscribe. Most anarchist bombings in Spain were clearly reprisals carried out by small groups or individuals rather than instrumental acts designed to weaken or topple the government (one exception was the foiled plan by a Frenchman and a Portuguese to blow up the Spanish parliament in 1892). More typical of anarchist action was the sequence of events leading from the May Day demonstrations of 1890 and 1891 to the Jerez uprising of January 1892, and thence to terrorist attacks to protest the execution of the ringleaders of the uprising. The Second Socialist International, meeting in Paris in July 1889, designated May 1 a day when the workers of all countries would celebrate labor and demand the eight-hour workday. May Day and the eight-hour day were in turn closely tied to the memory of the Haymarket Affair in the United States, in which a bomb was thrown during an anarchist demonstration in Chicago, 4 May 1886, killing a policeman and leading to further bloodshed between police and the crowd. The police arrested many prominent local anarchists, and the state executed four of them the following year on slender evidence. The anarchists' speeches at their trial and their martyrdom for the cause created a worldwide stir.

While the socialists intended to use the new workers' day for peaceful celebrations, the anarchists feared May Day's routinization and hoped to use it to spark confrontations with the authorities. They viewed the eight-hour issue as potentially revolutionary rather than reformist, both because it preserved the memory of the Haymarket martyrs and because it would give the workers more leisure time in which to contemplate and organize for social revolt. After crowds formed to celebrate the first May Day in Andalusia, the police vowed to disrupt the second one, shutting down the major anarchist newspaper of the region and jailing its editor, the beloved Fermin Salvochea, who played the role of anarchist "saint" in Spain, as Kropotkin did internationally. These acts only spurred the demonstrators; shortly after May Day in 1891 two bombs exploded in Cádiz. This led to mass arrests, including the rearrest of Salvochea, and the closing of the workers' centers in the city.

The police were always ready to assume that violent deeds were the product of conspiracies directed by anarchist leaders such as Salvochea. Either for this reason or simply as an excuse to suppress the movement, the Spanish authorities were especially prone to rounding up large numbers of anarchists on little or no evidence. Many of the anarchists they jailed were suspected of belonging to a secret society called La Mano Negra (The Black Hand), a group that may have been entirely a figment of the authorities' imaginations. On 8 January 1892, the jail in Jerez, in the heart of the wine-making country of Andalusia, still held 157 anarchists from the previous year's events. That night, several hundred workers and peasants armed with farm implements and sticks marched on the Jerez jail. On the way they killed two men, then laid siege to the prison, but they were easily dispersed the next day by a regiment of cavalry. Within a month numerous anarchists had been arrested and tried by the military for sedition. Many received long prison terms, including Fermin Salvochea, even though he had been incarcerated at the time of the uprising. Four anarchists were executed for the murder of the two *jerezanos*, but whether in fact this was a premeditated anarchist insurrection or merely a spontaneous riot has never been clearly established. The anarchists themselves viewed Jerez as an explosion of discontent and pointed out that the crude nature of the workers' weapons and the lack of any attempt to cut telegraph lines or railroad tracks made it unlikely that this had been a carefully planned rebellion.[7]

What is clear is that the perception of injustice was perpetuated by the heavy hand of the military and the police. The following year a thirty-year-old emigrant from South America named Paulino Pallas decided to avenge the "judicial murders" of the Andalusian anarchists by killing the captain general of Barcelona, Martínez de Campos. The bomb he threw killed the general's horse and several others, but not the general. Within a month, Pallas's own quick execution was avenged (as he had foretold in his last words) by a friend, in a particularly horrible way. Santiago Salvador threw two bombs from the fifth floor of Barcelona's Liceo Opera House into the seats below, which were filled with mostly upper-class operagoers, killing at least fifteen and wounding many more. This is how he explained his deed: "The death of Pallas produced in me a terrible feeling, and in order to avenge his death, as a tribute to his memory, I conceived of a plan in which it was possible to terrorize those who had enjoyed killing him and who believed that they had nothing to fear. . . . I only meditated about the form of the deed; it had to be something that would make a great deal of noise."[8] Salvador confessed to the crime when apprehended, but the police refused to believe that he had acted alone, as he maintained, and tortured several other anarchists into confessing that they had been part of the plot. The authorities executed six other anarchists as well as Salvador, and sentenced four to prison for life.

Spain underwent one further cycle of violence during this era of bombings. During the festival of Corpus Christi in June 1896, a bomb was thrown at the ecclesiastical and military dignitaries parading through the streets of Barcelona, killing six and injuring at least forty-five bystanders. The fact that most of the victims were common people marching at the end of the parade led the anarchists to suspect an agent provocateur or else some amateur. The real perpetrator was never identified, but the military responded with a ferocity that revived memories of the black legend of inquisitorial cruelty. Of 300 anarchists arrested, the lucky ones were deported without trial to Africa. Eighty-seven others were subjected to atrocious conditions, including torture, in Montjuich fortress overlooking the city. Their plight drew international attention; nevertheless, seventy-five of the prisoners were convicted, most receiving long prison terms and five being garroted in the prison courtyard. Given the notoriety of the affair, no one was surprised when the Spanish prime minister, Antonio Cánovas del Castillo, was assassinated in 1897. He was killed not by a Spaniard but by an Italian anarchist named Angiolillo who had lived in Barcelona.

In the severe repression of these years, many anarchist intellectuals and leaders fled abroad. Yet the movement began to revive as early as 1898, in the wake of Spain's humiliating defeat in the Spanish-American War and the loss of the remnants of the once grand colonial empire. New journals were published and intellectual and literary anarchism reached new peaks, demonstrating that the wave of violence had not dampened enthusiasm for anarchist ideas among progressive members of the urban middle classes. What seems clear about anarchism internationally is that key figures in the movement came to reevaluate their earlier assent to the doctrine of propaganda by the deed, which had linked the movement to terrorist tactics and brought down the wrath of governments without advancing the position of the masses. Responsible figures, such as Ricardo Mella and Anselmo Lorenzo in Spain, did not embrace the Nietzschean tendencies of café anarchism, but they did see a way out of the terrorist impasse. Meanwhile, a more liberal governmental attitude allowed the proliferation of anarchist publications as well as labor unions.

Historians have tended to focus on the development of anarcho-syndicalism as the primary anarchist response to the terrorist impasse of the end of the century. Conversely, they have sometimes viewed experiments in communal living, vegetarianism, and Esperanto, and other attempts to embody positive libertarian principles, as dispersing the energies of the movement. Because of the organizational weakness of their movement, anarchists had always been inclined toward a broadly cultural approach to politics that encouraged working-class solidarity and raised peoples' consciousness of their oppression. In such relatively tolerant periods as that between 1898 and 1914, and again after the declaration of the Second Republic in 1931, there arose in Spain not only an anarchist press, but also schools, communes, neighborhood cultural centers, libraries, and theater groups. Some of these were affiliated with the unions; all functioned to impart a community spirit that the workplace-oriented unions were unable to provide. Women and children especially were likely to be excluded from the union ranks and certainly from union leadership, and women were therefore particularly active in the *ateneos,* or cultural centers. Since the CNT was not founded until 1910, the anarchist schools and community centers actually preceded anarchist labor organizations. In both cases, the Spanish followed the example of French anarchists, since the French anarcho-syndicalist movement preceded the Spanish by about fifteen years. Francisco Ferrer opened his Escuela Moderna in Barcelona in 1901, after having spent many years living in Paris, where he was influenced by such educational reformers as Paul Robin. Although the authorities closed down his rationalist school in 1906, it spawned numerous imitators all over Spain. In the early years of the twentieth century, anarchists were experimenting with institutions that expressed their values of mutuality and self-development. These experiments would reach their full fruition in Spain in the 1930s.

Anarcho-syndicalism and World War I

Spain followed a pattern of anarchist development similar to that of the rest of Europe, especially France. Where it diverged was in expanding rather than contracting its activities after 1914. French workers and union leaders had found themselves faced with the prospect of either opposing French entry into World War I at the cost of government repression and political isolation, or else acquiescing to the kind of conflict they had been condemning for decades. They may have had no choice but to participate in the general mobilization, but French anarchism never recovered from the militarization of French society. Spain, however, remained neutral during World War I, while the workers became embittered by the effect of inflation and continued low wages.

The Spanish government had wisely refrained from feverish alliance-making, unlike the rest of Europe; besides, Spain had already had a taste of the disasters of war in 1898 and again in 1909, after an embarrassing defeat in Morocco. On that latter occasion the government had tried to call up Catalonian reservists for service in Africa. The response had been insurrection in Barcelona, leading to the Semana Tragica of July 1909, which featured intense anticlericalism as well as hostility toward Madrid. In the aftermath there was the usual wave of arrests, deportations, and executions, including that of the educator Francisco Ferrer, which provoked an international outcry. The anarchists had not in fact led the spontaneous antimilitarist uprising, but they were so closely associated with this sort of movement that the government assumed they were to blame. The workers' response to the carnage and the resulting repression was to reject further political involvement and to join the antipolitical CNT, which formed the following year. On the eve of World War I, the peasants and agricultural laborers were organizing *sindicatos*, or unions.

Labor was relatively quiet during the first years of the war, enjoying an economic boom as the reward for Spanish neutrality. From the restoration of the monarchy in the 1870s until 1910, for example, the percentage of the population engaged in the three economic sectors had remained unchanged, but from 1910 to 1930 the number of farmers declined by 20 percent, to less than 50 percent of the population, while the industrial and service sectors each increased by 10 percent. By 1917, however, inflation had far outstripped wage increases, while the full-employment situation had given the workers a greater sense of their potential power.

Then came the Russian Revolution, which fired the messianic ideals of the anarchists: not until 1921 and 1922 did they come to agree with Emma Goldman and other anarchists that the Bolshevik Revolution had betrayed libertarian ideals. Immediately after the war the anarchists took a similar stance to that held in the late 1860s, when they had tried to adhere to the ideas of Bakunin as well as to the First International. By 1922, however, the CNT rejected the Comintern and chose to send delegates instead to a new syndicalist international being founded in Berlin. The anarcho-syndicalists emerged from the First World War with their strength greatly increased and their revolutionary enthusiasm heightened. The only question would be what form their action would take: terrorist, insurrectionary, or syndicalist?

Some remarkable syndicalist leaders emerged in this period to urge a relatively moderate and pragmatic approach. Most notable among them was Salvador Segui, who dreamed of unifying the CNT unions with those of the socialist Unión General de Trabajadores (UGT) so as to enroll all Spanish workers in one powerful organization. Like his French counterpart, Fernand Pelloutier, Segui was that rarity among anarchists, a talented organizer who aspired to some degree of centralized organization and encouraged limited goals, such as legal status and the eight-hour day. Naturally he aroused the ire of pure anarchists who feared creeping reformism.

Meanwhile the syndicalists experienced some victories during the wave of strikes that spread through Spain in 1919, especially at the large Barcelona electrical plant called La Canadiense. After a general strike in the spring of 1919, the workers won their eight-hour day and management recognition of their unions. Success led them to strike again to obtain the release of their imprisoned comrades, but the government retaliated against the strike committees, arresting many more. By the winter of 1919-20 the employers responded to strikes with long lockouts of their workers, attitudes become polarized, and violence escalated on both sides. The employers hired pistoleros to brutalize the workers; the anarchists formed action groups to strike back. Conservative Premier Eduardo Dato was one of 1,500 people killed on both sides between 1919 and 1923, with 900 killed in Barcelona alone. Finally Segui was cut down in 1923; a group called Solidarios retaliated by killing the Archbishop of Saragossa. All this was taking place while anarchists and syndicalists were being arrested en masse. Finally in September 1923, a little less than a year after Mussolini came to power in Italy, the disorder ended with the typically Spanish device of a *pronunciamiento,* or military coup.

After General Miguel Primo de Rivera came to power, the CNT was outlawed and went underground. At the same time the general cleverly made overtures to the socialist union, even placing their leader Francisco Largo Caballero on his council of state. This attempt to wean the workers away from anarchism failed, however, since Primo de Rivera was dependent on the support of the army and the large landowners, and heavily favored the church throughout his seven-year regime. He also severely suppressed even the mildest forms of Catalan autonomy, which led the people of Catalonia, when given the chance, to vote overwhelmingly for a republican form of government. When the general's regime lost the support of the middle as well as the lower classes, the king demanded his resignation in January 1930.

In 1930 Spain parted from the rising authoritarian tide that engulfed much of Europe, including neighbor Portugal under Antonio de Oliveira Salazar. Elections were finally held in 1931 in which the people firmly announced their preference for a republic. King Alfonso XIII departed reluctantly after it became clear that the army would not prop up his reign, and thus began the tumultuous period of the Second Spanish Republic. The anarchists were already conspiring to bring about the social revolution.

CNT and FAI

The CNT was once again legalized in 1931 and that year held its first national congress since 1919. Four hundred delegates attended, representing over half a million members, and the union leaders urged cooperation with the new republican government. Again the moderates were opposed by the pure anarchists. In 1927, during the dictatorship of General Primo de Rivera, about fifty anarchists had met near Valencia to organize a Bakunin-style secret society. They called it the Federación Anarquista Ibérica, or FAI, to emphasize the union of Spanish and Portuguese anarchists, and saw themselves as a revolutionary elite that would infiltrate and lead the large and necessarily less doctrinaire organizations such as the CNT. All of the *faístas*, as they were called, also belonged to the CNT, but many of the syndicalist leadership opposed FAI influence on the union. In September 1931 the moderates within the CNT issued a statement declaring that impulsive revolutionism would only bring on fascism in Spain. The *faístas* responded by seizing the offices of the syndicalist newspaper *Solidaridad Obrera*, forcing out such relatively moderate syndicalists as Angel Pestaña and Juan Peiró, head of the CNT and editor of the newspaper, respectively.[10]

After the dark years of dictatorship and suppression, one might have expected the anarchists to have welcomed the advent of another Spanish republic as an opportunity to pursue agrarian and industrial reform and greater regional autonomy. This may have been the attitude of the moderates, but the members of FAI saw only a greater opportunity for encouraging social revolution. Their antagonism to the republican government of Manuel Azaña y Diaz was heightened by the growing spirit of class conflict brought on by the worldwide depression. Furthermore, the socialist minister of labor in the new government, Largo Caballero, instituted a series of new laws in 1931 that greatly increased the role of government in adjudicating labor disputes. Boards were set up with the power to impose binding arbitration, and unions were required to give eight days' notice before calling a strike. The new officials were mostly socialists, whose aim was to extend the influence of the socialist union, the UGT, at the expense of the anarcho-syndicalist CNT. The anarchists of FAI were not likely to welcome this new state of affairs. Anarchist intransigence and rising unemployment led to a variety of insurrections and general strikes. The most famous anarchist uprisings of these pre-civil war years demonstrate the continuing conflict between syndicalist and insurrectionary approaches to anarchism.

The FAI was organized into revolutionary cells called affinity groups, usually numbering only a handful of activists each to discourage penetration of the organization by the authorities. The most important of these groups was the Barcelona-based group, the Indomitables, because it included the already legendary bank robbers and terrorists Buenaventura Durruti and Francisco Ascaso, and the important organizer, Juan García Oliver. Their ongoing policy was to take advantage of worker unrest to create situations of revolutionary confrontation. The Indomitables' first major attempt to produce an explosion of this kind occurred in the Llobregat Valley mining district of Catalonia in January 1932. They failed to coordinate their uprising with the activities of the workers, however, and by the time they mounted a general strike the uprising had already been crushed. The republican government rounded up Durruti, Ascaso, and a hundred other militants and deported them without trial, but after considerable agitation and some threats they were returned to Barcelona by the end of the year. Undeterred by this failure, the Indomitables appeared eager to live up to their name. The spirit of revolutionary adventurism embodied in Bakunin in the 1860s and in Malatesta in the 1870s was alive and well in 1930s Spain.

The Barcelona *faístas* immediately began planning another conjunction of general strike and violent insurrection, this time based on a threatened strike by the railway workers' union. García Oliver hypothesized that if the railways were disabled, the government would be immobilized. If the anarchists all over Spain could be convinced to rise up simultaneously, tying down local detachments of civil guards and soldiers, the key urban centers might fall and the revolution be won. To counter the lack of centralized control that was fundamental to their anarchist spirit, the national committee of the FAI decreed in late December 1932 that "whichever region raises the flag of revolt, all other regions must follow in line and commit themselves equally to the revolt."[11] This ruling allowed a single regional group to initiate action that the entire membership would be obligated to follow. Extremist audacity preempted CNT moderation.

The Barcelona *faístas* set 8 January 1933 as the date for their insurrection. They had been storing weapons in hidden caches, some of which had been uncovered by the police, and they feared that a delay of their plans would threaten their arsenals. The railway workers had set 8 January for their strike, but instead of striking they settled for a small pay raise. Just as at Llobregat, the impetuous *faístas* jumped the gun, and the trains carried the government's troops where they were needed to put down the uprisings. Clashes took place at many major cities. A train was derailed in Valencia, and in the nearby town of Ribarroja the anarchists actually managed to take over the town hall and burn the archives. The director general of security, Arturo Menéndez, authorized the unrestricted use of force to put down the uprisings, and by the next day it was clear that the *faístas* had failed. Not only had the workers not cooperated by calling a general strike, but also the populace largely stayed indoors and left the militants on their own. Nevertheless, the violence spread to the southern province of Cádiz June tenth, and the government shifted its force of assault guards (a new republican complement to the civil guard, created in 1931) south from Madrid by railroad. The insurrection that had begun in the north would strike most tragically in a small Andalusian town called Casas Viejas.[12]

Casas Viejas

Historians, most notably Eric Hobsbawm, have tried to cite the Casas Viejas uprising as an example of the primitive millenarian appeal of anarchism to the backward Spanish peasantry. The *campesinos* were often illiterate, but they did not engage in combat with a millenarian fervor. Rather, they responded to the call to revolt from faraway Barcelona, and many of them embarked on their insurrectionary course with the greatest reluctance; in fact some of the leaders of the syndicate refused to join in at all. Nor were they mesmerized by a charismatic leader. Seventy-three-year-old Seisdedos, usually portrayed as a John Brown–like leader, was not even involved in the events, and there was no figure who commanded great authority in the community. The peasants were naïve, but they were not utopian visionaries.

An anarchist *sindicato* had first been organized in Casas Viejas in 1914, when an activist and charcoal burner by trade moved there with his *compañera*, or female companion, and three children, seeking work. He organized the landless agricultural workers of the town, encouraging literacy and moderation in drink as well as economic betterment. Anarchism had gone underground during the 1920s, but enthusiasm for it resurfaced after the declaration of the republic in 1931. Wages were low and life was very hard in Casas Viejas; increased expectations had not been met by any significant social change. The leaders of the local *sindicato* were notified of the planned insurrection, but were told to await word of success elsewhere before committing their men to revolt. The local schoolteacher owned a radio, and the strike leaders heard that the revolt had failed but did not believe the reports. A note from Jerez reached the town, calling for them to strike at 10 P.M. on 10 January. The anarchists debated what to do, with the older men urging caution and the younger ones wanting to man the barricades. They gathered outside of the town to await a signal light from a town nearby, but the signal never came (civil guards had dispersed the campesinos there before they could act). Nevertheless the head of the union issued orders to begin the takeover of Casas Viejas and its conversion to *communismo libertario*. Telephone wires linking the town to the outside world were cut and a trench was dug to prevent vehicles from entering by road. Some men guarded the crossroads, while others besieged the local barracks, which housed four civil guards. The anarchists were armed with shotguns that they normally used for hunting small game, and they raided a local shop to obtain cartridges and powder.

By dawn the next morning, a young woman known as La Libertaria was parading through town carrying the black and red flag of the CNT that had hung in their union hall, while the men marched with their shotguns and pistols, or even with hoes and pruning axes. Since there was no town hall, they burned the petty tax records, and advised the deputy mayor that if the civil guards stayed in their barracks they would not be hurt. The guards refused to bow to the peasants' demands, firing ensued, and two of the four guards were killed. Soon the telephone operator in the nearby town of Medina Sidonia reported that the phone lines were not operating and that the mail truck had not arrived. A detachment of civil guards accompanied a repairman to Casas Viejas, repaired the lines and captured the men that were guarding the crossroads. They requested reinforcements, which arrived that afternoon in the form of a dozen assault guards.

When the anarchists in the town heard of the capture of their *compañeros,* many panicked and fled into the surrounding countryside before the soldiers arrived. But some stayed, including the two marksmen who had shot the soldiers. They hid in the hut of their aged father, Curro Cruz, nicknamed Seisdedos or Six-fingers. From there they held the guards in a standoff into the night, while their friends fired from nearby rooftops. One guard was killed and another severely wounded, and reinforcements were brought in with machine guns and grenades. The mud walls of the hut provided no defense against these weapons, and the old man and his two sons were killed; the other occupants of the hut were forced out when the thatched roof was set on fire. The Casas Viejas insurrection was over.

The next morning the two remaining local civil guards escorted the soldiers through the town, rounding up a dozen young men who had not fled. They were taken to Seisdedos's hut, where the sight of the fire-consumed corpse of a dead guard so enraged the soldiers that they shot the unarmed detainees. This atrocity was not reported for two months, but when the details of the savage repression finally did come out, they created a loss of confidence in the government of Manuel Azaña that contributed to his resignation nine months after the confrontation at Casas Viejas. The officer in charge of the assault guards was tried the following year and sentenced to twenty-one years in prison, though the civil war aborted his sentence.

In the aftermath of the failed revolt, the moderate elements of the CNT condemned the revolutionary adventurists of the FAI. Already on 9 January the syndicalist newspaper, *CNT,* had written:

> Our revolution is not a mere plot; we do not arrive at our ends through conspiracy. (Our revolution) concerns the elevation of the proletarian conscience. It involves the organization when their potential reaches its maximum, and when the central organization—not the (local) committees—determine it. . . . Our revolution does not consist of an assault on a civil guard barracks or army post. That is not revolutionary. We will declare a general strike when we can count on the greatest possibility of success; when we can take

over factories, mines, electrical centers, transportation. . . .
That cannot be done secretly. The preparation must be done
publicly, in the light of day.[13]

It was unfortunate that the anarchists of Casas Viejas could not have
read this editorial before they committed themselves to their hopeless uprising. Most of the local anarchists who had fled the town
were eventually rounded up and given jail sentences. For their part,
the Barcelona militants accepted their responsibility for the uprising
proudly, and tried to enroll the twenty dead *campesinos* of Casas
Viejas as martyrs whose example should encourage others to rebel.

Decline of the Second Republic

In the next two years the situation for the Spanish Republic went
from bad to worse. The coalition of leftist parties fragmented in 1933,
and the conservatives came to power at the end of the year. This
political shift led the socialists to adopt militant tactics formerly
associated only with the anarcho-syndicalists. Black January 1933
was followed by Red October 1934 when, in a far more serious
rebellion, the miners of Asturias rose against the government. Most
participants were socialists; the anarchists played a subsidiary but
enthusiastic role. Thirty thousand armed workers held off the army
for two weeks, until the government took the unprecedented step of
sending in Moorish troops from North Africa to put down the
Spanish workers. In bloody fighting 1,200 workers were killed.
Afterwards, the government arrested 20,000 workers and executed
many of them. It also raided anarchist centers and closed down their
newspapers. The FAI perpetrated no more revolts against the
increasingly conservative republic.[14]

The political response was a renewed search by republican leader
Manuel Azaña for a coalition on the left. In 1935 the Popular Front
coalition of republican parties was eventually extended to include
the socialists, and soon Joseph Stalin, eager to stem the fascist tide in
Europe, would encourage the participation of the fledgling communist party as well. The CNT/FAI had counselled abstention from
voting in 1933; in the crucial elections of 1936 their supporters
provided enough votes to ensure the victory of the Popular Front.
Their main inducement was the prospect of the release of the many
anarchist political prisoners. Still, any anarchist support for electoral

politics was controversial. The *faísta* theorist Diego Abad de Santillán openly acknowledged that the anarchists chose a policy of supporting the lesser evil, fearful of the advent of fascism if the right won. As the very real threat from the right increased to the point of civil war, the anarchists would be forced to reassess many of their long-cherished positions.

Between the election of February 1936 and the military uprising of July, Spain was rocked by violence and incipient social revolution. Peasants began to occupy hundreds of thousands of acres of land, especially in the south and east. Both the UGT and the CNT called numerous strikes throughout the spring that paralyzed the major cities. Street battles erupted between paramilitary forces organized by the fascist Falange and the socialist and anarchist left. The government tried to arrest both Falangists and anarchists but proved powerless to contain the violence. Azaña seemed most concerned with preventing the socialists from taking over his government. In the midst of this turmoil, the anarcho-syndicalists met at a national congress of the CNT in Saragossa in May. Six hundred fifty delegates represented over half a million workers. All felt that Spain was on the verge of revolution, so their discussions had an unusual urgency. The schisms within the CNT were healed, an anarchist militia was formed to defend the movement, and villagers were urged to seize lands belonging to absentee landlords. But before the anarchists could organize a unified revolution, the Falangists attempted their own. The murder of a prominent right-wing politician on 12 July hastened the Falangist generals' decision to act. On 17 July 1936, General Francisco Franco flew to Morocco to take control of the Spanish army stationed there, and the next day army garrisons throughout Spain attempted to seize control of the cities. The Spanish civil war had begun.

The Spanish Civil War

The army succeeded in taking several key cities and regions during the opening days of the rebellion, but failed to get control of the three major cities of Spain: Madrid, Barcelona, and Valencia. By late summer of 1936, as troops crossed over from Africa and headed north, Franco's forces controlled most of the south and west of the country, while the Popular Front government remained strong in the east, in Aragon, Catalonia, Valencia, and Murcia. The first great victory for the anarchists came in Barcelona, where they defeated the army in pitched battles on 19 and 20 July. Buenaventura Durruti emerged as the anarchist military commander; his close friend Francisco Ascaso was killed at the end of the fighting for the city. The rebellion in fact created the kind of social revolution that the anarchists had discussed at their Saragossa conference two months before (Saragossa itself fell to the nationalist forces, as the rightist military leaders called themselves). Catalonia and Aragon were controlled by the unions much more than by the central government, which was ensconced first in Madrid and later in Valencia.

From July 1936 until May 1937 the anarcho-syndicalists worked to prosecute the war and simultaneously to realize their long-held dreams of social revolution. Nestor Makhno had been faced with a similar situation during the civil war in Russia, but unlike the Ukraine, Catalonia was one of the most advanced industrial regions of Spain, and anarchists were much better organized there. By the end of 1936 the CNT, for example, claimed 3 million adherents. This period in Spain offers a unique glimpse of anarchism in action, albeit one never freed from the rigors of pursuing a war against a better-equipped and professionally led army. How well could anarchists measure up to the challenge? Given the situation of civil war, this question must be divided into military and civilian responses to the crisis.

To defend their territory, the anarchists, socialists, Catalan regionalists, and Marxists created militias made up of volunteers who were usually linked ideologically. The anarchists were particularly notorious for eschewing rank and military discipline, and for deciding as democratically as possible when and where to attack. Long on front line soldiers and short on logistics and supplies, they lacked the experienced officer corps enjoyed by the nationalists. They also lacked support from the government in Madrid, which was initially dominated by left-wing republicans who trusted neither anarchist revolutionaries nor Catalan autonomists. The anarchists have been criticized for having been wasteful and inefficient in their use of resources. The supply situation became so critical that anarchist commander Durruti was forced to employ a portion of his forces in making weapons at the front.[15]

The anarchists always insisted on linking the war and the revolution. The anarchist militias had to overcome an inherent antimilitary bias and hoped to make up in enthusiasm what they lacked in professionalism, training, and discipline. Yet by the fall of 1936 the anarchist leaders were instituting more formal discipline and even some semblance of military hierarchy, though Durruti refused an officer's commission. Because the war was lost by the regular republican army long after it had absorbed the militias, it is difficult to evaluate anarchist claims of effectiveness. The record in 1936 suggests that the militias were most effective defensively, as in the heroic defense of Madrid that cost Durruti his life in November. They tended to lack the coordination and sustained drive necessary for offensive warfare, so that even with numerical superiority they proved unable to liberate the Aragonese towns of Huesca and Saragossa.[16] In any case, the outcome of the war was largely determined by the military aid given by Nazi Germany and Fascist Italy to the nationalists and by Soviet Russia to the loyalist forces over which they exercised control; none of the aid was available to the anarchists.

Most striking to the foreigners who flocked to Spain to observe or join the revolution was the transformation of Barcelona after the revolution of 19 July. In frequently cited passages at the beginning of his book on the Spanish civil war, *Homage to Catalonia,* George Orwell described the city as it appeared to him on his arrival in December 1936.

> When one came straight from England the aspect of Barcelona was something startling and overwhelming. It was the first time that I had ever been in a town where the working class was in the saddle. Practically every building of any size was draped with red flags or with the red and black flag of the Anarchists. . . . almost every church had been gutted and its images burnt. . . . Every shop and café had an inscription saying that it had been collectivized; even the bootblacks had been collectivized and their boxes painted red and black. Waiters and shop-walkers looked you in the face and treated you as an equal. Servile and even ceremonial forms of speech had temporarily disappeared. Nobody said "Señor" or "Don" or even "Usted;" everyone called everyone else "Comrade" and "Thou," and said "Salud!" instead of "Buenos dias. . . . "Down the Ramblas, the wide central artery of the town where crowds of people streamed constantly to and fro, the loud-speakers were bellowing revolutionary songs all day and far into the night. And it was the aspect of the crowds that was the queerest thing of

all. In outward appearance it was a town in which the wealthy classes had practically ceased to exist. Except for a small number of women and foreigners there were no "well-dressed" people at all. Practically everyone wore rough working-class clothes, or blue overalls or some variant of the militia uniform. All this was queer and moving. There was much in it that I did not understand, in some ways I did not even like it, but I recognized it immediately as a state of affairs worth fighting for.[17]

Orwell did fight, not with the anarchists but with an anti-Stalinist Marxist group called the Partido Obrero de Unificación Marxista (POUM), which the Russian communists stigmatized as Trotskyist and which they succeeded in suppressing later in 1937. Orwell also realized that the bourgeoisie had not really disappeared but was simply keeping itself inconspicuous. Still, the libertarian communism he experienced in Catalonia always remained for Orwell a model of what might be achieved if socialism were not corrupted by the totalitarian form practiced by Stalin.

Libertarian Communism

Libertarian communism meant control of the means of production by the workers themselves. In practice this took many forms, as workers' committees controlled some factories and unions some others; still other were run by workers' committees in conjunction with government agencies (since government was often bypassed but not abolished). Nevertheless, workers did take control of both large and small enterprises, and they did not show a crafts bias; in fact they sometimes closed down inefficient businesses so as to concentrate production in larger and more modern enterprises, thus simplifying the regulation and coordination of production. All factories employing over 100 workers, and those whose owners had fled, were collectivized without compensation; those with 50 to 100 workers could be collectivized on the vote of two-thirds of the employees. Small-scale enterprises were sometimes forcibly collectivized, as with the Barcelona dairies, or the owners were simply forced by the union to take on extra workers.

Barcelona led the way in establishing an anarchist social and cultural infrastructure. Within a week of the revolutionary triumph of July, a New Unified School System appeared under the direction of Juan Puig Elias, president of the cultural section of the CNT and director of the Escuela Natura. A Popular University was installed on the premises of a former French convent, with books requisitioned from all over the city. The closing of Catholic institutions created a need for nurse training programs to replace the nuns who had dominated nursing, and for secular hospitals. At the Casa de la Dona Treballadora, women were trained as nurses as well as for other professions. In Barcelona, the Casa de Maternidad provided birth and postnatal care and strongly encouraged breastfeeding. At the same time abortion was legalized and divorce, of course, became available as anarchists avoided both church and state sanctification of free unions. Into the breach stepped the unions to formalize the marital state, but anarchist women mocked this adaptation of traditional practices and argued for purely consensual unions between free adults.

The women who spoke out on behalf of equality of the sexes and greater female participation in the workforce and in society were part of a new organization, founded just prior to the civil war, called Mujeres Libres, or Free Women. Other leftist groups also formed women's groups, but whereas the communists emphasized utilizing women in the common fight against fascism by putting them in men's places in the fields and factories so that the men could fight at the front, the anarchist women went beyond this functional approach to argue for the empowerment of women throughout the public and private spheres. Some anarchist women, such as Federica Montseny, were not inclined to speak of feminism, feeling that feminists simply wanted to open up more places for women in the capitalist world, and preferred to speak instead of integral humanism. But the women who organized Mujeres Libres and published its newspaper strongly believed in the need for an autonomous women's movement within the anarchist ranks, since even anarchist men too often accepted the traditional subservience of Spanish women. They fought against the triple enslavement of women to ignorance, to production, and to gender-based discrimination, and they particularly emphasized the importance of education and consciousness raising.[18]

The anarchists were equally enthusiastic about rural collectivization, and the rapidity and scope of the rural revolution they introduced was remarkable: three-fourths of all the land in Aragon, half of Catalonia and the Levante were collectivized. Over 5.5 million hectares were divided between 1,200 and 1,700 communes. Not all peasants were eager to join collectives of course, and some Catalonian smallholders created their own agricultural union. One reason that Aragon was so highly collectivized was that Durruti's columns forcibly encouraged the process as they marched through the province. The anarchists believed that small-scale, private production was inefficient and reinforced a retrograde egoist mentality, so despite earlier peasant dreams of a *reparto*, collectivization rather than redistribution of land was the rule. Since most agricultural workers lived in towns, the collectives usually encompassed either entire towns or large portions of them.

These were not communes made up of a few families—in Aragon, the average collective numbered 960 members. Each collective had a general assembly of the members and an administrative council that served as an executive body. The collectives seem generally to have increased food production during the civil war. They voluntarily brought food to the soldiers at the front. Supplying the cities proved a greater problem, however, and distribution and coordination were much thornier problems for the anarchists than was production itself. Nor was there any effective way of reallocating resources from wealthier to poorer collectives, other than through moral exhortation. Within the collectives many members set up pension funds for widows, orphans, and invalids, which was a tremendous improvement over the old society.[19]

Life in a libertarian commune departed most dramatically from that in the old society with the abolition of money, since "money and power are diabolical philters that turn a man into a wolf, into a rabid enemy, instead of into a brother."[20] At the most extreme, villagers simply received provisions from the local store, but more typically each family received vouchers that could be exchanged for basic commodities. Pay was thus allocated by family size rather than by function. Services could also be paid for in coupons, since local doctors, dentists, barbers, and tailors also were usually incorporated in the collective system. Everywhere, churches were converted into schools, dining halls, and cafés. Money was still necessary for transactions that involved the outside world, and for this currency the *campesino* had to petition the executive committeee, which had complete control of all the monetary resources of the collective. (Executive committee members rotated on a regular basis.)

Outside observers commonly inquired whether having to petition the committee every time the *campesinos* wanted to go into town infringed on their freedom. They also noted the frequent absence of such "luxuries" as bars serving liquor—and even cafés serving coffee, in some particularly abstemious collectives. Tobacco was frowned upon, and brothels were closed. Rural anarchism was profoundly moralistic; revolutionary virtue was defined as the absence of egotistical bourgeois pleasures. But most members of the collective seemed bemused by these questions; certainly they were free to go into town, they said, but not to engage in vice![21]

Evaluating the success of this revolution is made difficult by its short duration, by the ongoing war, and above all by the anarchists' Popular Front "allies'" efforts to destroy it. Capital flight hampered investment; scarcity of resources hindered cooperation between collective enterprises. In terms of overall production, steel and truck manufacturing declined while textiles and dairy production actually increased. Most industries held steady or declined slightly, but the increased production of bullets, shells, and gunpowder for the military was impressive. The anarchists claimed great success on the moral plane, in enhancing the downtrodden peasants' dignity and the workers' solidarity. This is what so inspired Orwell: that despite economic hardships—there were already breadlines by the winter of 1936—there was a spirit of equality and freedom, and there were virtually no beggars. At least one can safely assert that the loss of the civil war in 1938 and 1939 was not due to the social revolution of 1936 and 1937.[22]

The anarchists and anarcho-syndicalists had always envisioned a strictly social revolution, having assumed that after the collapse of the bourgeois state, government could be dispensed with entirely. The situation they faced in 1936 was thus unforeseen, for the revolution had been handed to them by a counterrevolution, forcing them to cooperate with other progressive political forces to defeat Franco. Initially they tried to abide by their principles, creating democratic militias rather than a hierarchically ordered army and governing by committee rather than through ministers and parliaments. Their two main revolutionary committees were the Anti-Fascist Militia Committee, composed of socialists, communists, and Catalan regionalists, as well as representatives of the CNT and FAI, and the Catalan Economic Council. Soon a Council of Aragon also emerged to oversee territory conquered by the militias. Within the anarchist ranks debate immediately broke out over cooperation with the Catalan regional government of Luis Companys and with the national government centered in Madrid. The influential *faísta* Diego

Abad de Santillán wanted to establish a Council of National Defense, guided by council communism to replace the formal national government, and such a proposal was forwarded to Madrid in August, but there it was ignored. The head of the CNT, Horacio Prieto, and Federica Montseny advocated cooperating with the government as long as the war lasted. If the issue had been whether anarchists could cooperate with republicans and socialists, as they perhaps should have between 1931 and 1936, the problem would have been relatively simple. But by the summer of 1936 a new power equation existed, due to the growing influence of the communists.

Anarchists versus Communists

Numerically weak in Spain, the communists were the exact opposite of the mass-based and indigenous CNT-FAI—they were a disciplined party taking orders from Moscow. The communist party line after 1935 called for the creation of popular fronts to combat the threat of fascism, and therefore for cooperation with all progressive bourgeois and socialist parties (which Stalin had previously labeled "social fascists"). In the Spanish case, to appeal for aid from the Western democracies, both the loyalist government and the communist party wanted to downplay the revolutionary aspects of their fight against fascism. The communists thus ironically found supporters among the frightened middle classes, who saw communists as a bulwark against anarchist collectivization. They argued for the protection of private property, the necessity of centralized political power under a moderate republican government, and, above all, for the consolidation of the militias into a regular army. Their leverage was the offer of military aid from the Soviet Union. As it quickly became clear that Franco was receiving massive aid from Italy and Germany, it was this aid from the Soviet Union that tempted Federica Montseny and other anarchists into compromising their principles.

Yet without the militias, the revolution was defenseless; without the revolution, what were the anarchists fighting for? If the anarchists refused to collaborate with the central government and remained allied with the Catalan regionalists, they would be faced with a civil war within the civil war—hardly a recipe for success. This was to some degree the problem faced by the Basques, who had created their own autonomous region of Euzkadi and were loosely linked to the loyalists, although they remained fervent Catholics. The Basques were isolated and defeated by the nationalist forces in the spring of 1937, after sustaining a bloody invasion that included the incendiary bombing of Guernica by the German air force, an event made world famous by Picasso's painting.

The question of political participation facing the anarchists in 1936 and 1937 was the greatest crisis in their history. That formerly pure *faístas*, such as Montseny and Juan García Oliver, could compromise their principles sufficiently to join the government as ministers by the end of 1936 shows that they were willing to adapt their ideology to the exigencies of the situation. In September the moderate government in Madrid was replaced with one headed by the socialist Largo Caballero, "the Spanish Lenin," who sought Russian aid but resisted political control by the commissars. By October the military situation looked desperate, as Franco prepared to take Madrid. On 4 November four anarchists accepted portfolios in Largo Caballero's socialist government, and until the following May they linked their fortunes together in the joint struggle against both communism and fascism. Both groups would succumb the following year, the socialists being absorbed and the anarchists defeated by the communists' imperious demands for centralization of power and social control. But in the meantime, Federica Montseny became the first and only woman to achieve cabinet rank in Spain, becoming minister of health, and García Oliver became minister of justice; two CNT moderates were given the Industry and Commerce portfolios. Most Spanish anarchists seemed resigned to collaboration, although such foreign anarchists as Emma Goldman and the Italian Camillo Berneri argued against giving way to communist statism and reformism.

In November 1936, Madrid was saved from Franco's assault by a heroic defense made to the slogan "No Pasaran" (They Shall Not Pass). Yet the defense of the Spanish Republic faltered as Málaga in the south fell to the nationalists in February 1937. The moderate socialists, led by Indalecio Prieto, increasingly allied themselves with the communists against Largo Caballero, who consequently became more closely identified with his anarchist ministers and supporters.

More anarchists came into the government in lesser positions as the premier proved himself unwilling to accede to communist demands to dismantle the social revolution, and those already in more powerful positions did what they could to effect social change. The Ministers of Industry and Commerce, Juan Lopez Sánchez and Juan Peiró, defended the collectives against nationalization; García

Oliver radically reformed the administration of justice and set up Popular Tribunals instructed to consider human rights over property rights; Montseny made hundreds of speeches, set up wide-ranging public health projects, and worked to improve the rights and welfare of women and children. If this collaboration had been allowed to last, the history of anarchism might have been very different. The anarchist leaders seemed to be wedding their hopes for the oppressed with a more tempered appraisal of politics. The FAI was evolving into the political arm of the CNT, ready to take its place in a Popular Front parliament; it actually began to take such a role when the parliament reopened under the government of Juan Negrín in October 1937, and an anarchist from Asturias served in the Negrín government from April 1938 until the demise of the Republic. Yet 1937 was to sound the death knell of Spanish anarchism, as anarchists succumbed to attacks first by the communists and then by the nationalists.

The anarchists' very success in integrating themselves with the government of Largo Caballero contributed to their undoing. By the spring of 1937 the communists were increasingly disturbed by the anarchists' influence, and they found an unlikely ally in conservative Catalan regionalists who were tired of CNT/FAI control of Catalonia. A number of clashes between the two sides occurred that spring, culminating in a new Semana Tragica, the first week of May. Police sent by the Catalan government tried to wrest the Barcelona telephone exchange from anarchist control and were met by armed resistance. As the fighting spread, the communists built a barricade across from CNT/FAI headquarters on the Via Durruti and killed more than thirty defenders, despite the frantic attempts of Montseny and García Oliver to negotiate a ceasefire. Overall, five hundred anarchists were killed in the fighting, nearly half by communist assassination squads. Among the dead was Camillo Berneri; Montseny and García Oliver were saved only by heavy protection. The violence in Barcelona ended on 7 May, but anarchists were being attacked and killed elsewhere in Catalonia as well. In the aftermath of the fighting, the radical anarchist organization called the Friends of Durruti was proscribed, along with the allegedly Trotskyist POUM, and many of their members were rounded up as counter-revolutionaries. Communist assassins executed the POUM leader, Andrés Nin, and the communists threatened to suspend all aid unless the government of Largo Caballero resigned, which it did ten days later. For the next two years they controlled the more acquiescent government of Juan Negrín.

Subjugating the centralized state was easier than controlling the economy, but the communists did attempt to nationalize basic industries and even returned some plants to their previous owners to consolidate Catalan support, thus making good on the party declaration that "objective historical conditions do not permit a proletarian revolution."[23] The communist minister of agriculture was cautious about breaking up the collectives, fearing to disrupt their generally good record of food production, so he waited until after the harvest before trying to dismantle them. In August, the Negrín government dissolved the Council of Aragon and sent Enrique Líster's communist regiment to enforce dissolution of the local committees. The last anarchist stronghold fell 21 September 1937.[24] The social revolution was rolled back well before the collapse of the Spanish Republic. Berneri had argued that the success of the war depended on the success of the revolution. It is impossible to know to what degree loss of revolutionary enthusiasm contributed to the failures of the following year.

A great deal of ferocious and bloody fighting would take place after this "civil war within the civil war," until the fall of Barcelona in January 1939. The Spanish civil war became increasingly a foreign war, far less because of the International Brigades that fought with the Republic (after suffering tremendous losses, they were withdrawn in 1938) than because of communist and fascist aid and influence. Toward the end, the only hope of the Negrín government was that a general European war would break out and the British and French come belatedly to Negrín's aid as part of the overall offensive against fascism. The Munich Conference ended this possibility, both because of Western appeasement and because of Stalin's reevaluation of the international situation, which led him to shift from his alliance with the Popular Front to an accommodation with fascism. In a sense, even before the Nazi-Soviet Pact sealed the fate of Poland and ushered in World War II, an unwritten agreement had crushed the authentic social revolution of libertarian communism in Spain. Stalin could tolerate the self-determination of the workers and peasants no more than Franco or Hitler could.

After the defeat of the republic in 1939, the losers streamed over the border into France, where recriminations continued. Some anarchists stayed in France, many others emigrated to Mexico; the unluckiest were rounded up by Philippe Pétain's Vichy government and returned to Spain to face the firing squads. Back in Spain, repression was in full swing, and Spanish prisons were packed. Franco suppressed regionalism as fully as anarchism and ruled a rigidly centralized state with the blessing of a revived Catholic church.

Emma Goldman, who made the Spanish revolution the last great crusade of her life, died in 1940, deeply pessimistic about the future of her ideal. The dream of egalitarian liberty would continue, but the anarchist movement seemed dead, overwhelmed by the superior force of the totalitarian states.[25] George Orwell escaped from Spain in 1937 and discovered how difficult it was to expose Stalinist tactics in an England still enamored of the Marxist left. He would have no such difficulty a decade later, when he published *1984* on the eve of his own death. Though the Cold War would fashion the popular image of Orwell the anticommunist, the former imperial policeman never renounced the utopian vision of equality and freedom he encountered in anarchist Barcelona in 1936. The story Orwell and others had to tell—of how Spanish anarchism succumbed to the machinations of the communist party well before being over-whelmed by the right—encapsulates the century-long history of anarchism, from Proudhon's publication of *What Is Property?* in 1840 to the throngs of emigrés huddled in French internment camps, caught between the forces of Franco, Pétain, and Hitler in 1940. The anarchists' devotion to genuine popular revolution and to workers' control of the farms, factories, and workshops had profoundly threatened communist claims to represent the working class through state, party, and bureaucracy—otherwise called "the dictatorship of the proletariat." The international anarchy of warring states had no room for the social experiment called anarchism.

5

Contemporary Anarchism

Anarchism reached its apogee in Spain in July 1936; its demise as a large-scale movement can be dated from 1937. That it succumbed so rapidly to the communist onslaught reveals something about the anarchists' vulnerability to practitioners of power politics. At the meeting of the Anarchist International in Paris in 1937, the Spanish anarchists' compromises with government were condemned, despite arguments by Federica Montseny and the other *faístas* for the necessity of a politics of realism. By the eve of the Second World War, anarchism as a movement was already in disarray, and this new and even more horrible war further accelerated the influence of government over all aspects of society. After World War II came the rapid expansion of communist influence in the world, along with the Cold War. While Iberia remained repressed and isolated, Italy and France, formerly anarchist strongholds, felt the strong pull of communism, while more moderate socialists and laborites demanded a welfare state as the price of working-class sacrifice in the war.

Nevertheless, immediately after the war the venerable French anarchist newspaper *Le Libertaire* was still selling between sixty and eighty thousand copies a week, and even the British anarchist weekly *Freedom* was selling five thousand copies. Under the editorship of Albert Camus, the journal *Combat* had shed its adherence to the Communist party and was leaning toward the libertarian left. And a pro-anarchist group of painters called Art Libre held an exhibition in Paris in 1946 in which four hundred painters took part.[1]

Anarchism undoubtedly declined between 1914 and 1939, and it may never regain the revolutionary impact that it had earlier in this century. Yet anarchism has continued to evolve in the half-century since the Second World War, and it may still fill an important ideological niche in a world in which the approaching demise of communism—anarchism's great nemesis in the first half of the century—leaves little alternative to ascendant capitalism and political liberalism. The New Left of the 1960s has already demonstrated the greater appeal of anarchist over communist ideals for the postwar generation.

It was perhaps unfortunate for French philosopher Jean-Paul Sartre that anarchism had declined as a serious political force by the time he was seeking to reconcile the philosophy of existentialism with the need for political engagement in the modern world, for it would have been far easier to accommodate his thought to anarchism than to Soviet Marxism. Back at the turn of the century, numerous anarchists had found similar philosophical rapport with the ideas of Friedrich Nietzsche, who, like Sartre, proclaimed the need to engage oneself in the real world and not remain in some ivory tower, while at the same time to affirm one's individuality over all competing claims to one's identity. The central dilemma for the postwar existentialist was how to preserve one's freedom while committing oneself to social change. The existential stress on freedom and responsibility for one's own actions, on will and subjectivity, and at the same time on action rather than passivity are all themes reminiscent of anarchism, yet Sartre, somewhat perversely, struggled to connect his philosophy with communism as the only viable counterforce to capitalism. Meanwhile the other figure so often linked with existentialism, Camus, identified the ability to revolt, to say no to the objective situation, with the capacity to be human.

While Sartre alienated many of his fellow intellectuals with his attempt to marry existentialism to Marxism, the Communist party condemned the philosophy as nihilistic and subjectivist—in short, as bourgeois. Yet existentialism's anarchist implications were not lost on postwar intellectuals. The English anarchist Herbert Read agreed that the subjectivity of the individual, not abstractions or grandiose ideals, must be the starting point of all philosophy. He saw echoes of Max Stirner's egoism in Sartre's thought, with the major difference being that Sartre encouraged engagement in suprapersonal goals. To Read, Sartre's doctrine that "existence precedes essence" helped to correct the Rousseauistic notion that humans were "born free"; rather, said Read, they must create the condition of freedom.[2] The existentialist concept of the absurd accurately described Read's anarchist approach to politics. Facing the alternatives of government by the ignorant majority or by manipulative elites, he chose neither. Nor could Read find solace in the choice between accepting an unjust society or pinning one's hopes on the revolutionary installation of new elites in power. Instead he accepted Camus's distinction between revolution and rebellion. Spontaneous rebelliousness offered the only chance of affirming individual subjectivity over life-denying power structures. Rebellion was grounded in instinct rather than reason.

In company with such other English-speaking anarchists of the postwar era as George Woodcock, Paul Goodman, and Alex Comfort, Herbert Read advocated a neo-Romantic brand of anarchism. Intuition, creativity, and nonrepressive sexuality on the personal level, and permanent rebellion on the social level, liberated the individual from the lure of political revolution on the one hand and the status quo on the other. The ideal was a vision of personal and social wholeness that was strongly antitechnocratic. Read's notion of the "poeticization of all practicalities" drew upon the Romantics, such as Blake and Shelley, the anarchist aesthetes of the late nineteenth century, and the surrealists of the interwar era.[3] The Romantic denigration of reason would echo strongly in the 1960s.

The New Left and the Sixties

In the New Left's reappraisal in the 1960s of the heritage of the communist Old Left, anarchism reemerged as a significant force. The Communist party was identified with bureaucratic inertia and dogmatism, with rigid adherence to an outworn ideology, at the moment that a new generation of students sought alternatives to the military-industrial complex that was widely identified with the war to stamp out communism in Vietnam. The student revolt of the 1960s stretched from Berkeley to Paris to Amsterdam, from Tokyo to Mexico City. In Chicago in May 1969, a "radical decentralist" wing of Students for a Democratic Society (SDS) criticized the organization's Leninist tendencies. The anarchists feared SDS was becoming "an Old Left organization: elitist, bureaucratic, and centralized in structure, held together primarily by conventional programmatic issues" and advocated instead that their politics must be combined with life-style issues that would have an immediate appeal for their youthful constituents.[4] Yet as the United States escalated the bombing of Vietnamese peasants, SDS left the peace symbols to others and vowed to destroy the establishment, not in the name of anarchy but in solidarity with Ho Chi Minh, Mao Tse-tung, and Fidel Castro. The anti–Vietnam War movement placed a premium on antimilitarism and on identification with the plight of Third World peoples. Despite the centrality of opposition to the war, however, the familiar slogan of the 1960s was not "Make Peace, Not War," but rather "Make Love, not War." In the 1960s, love became political.

The antiwar movement met the youth counterculture, which explored subjective inner experience through mind-altering drugs, rock music, and mystical religious experience, and which redefined interpersonal relations through liberated social behavior, quintessentially expressed in the advocacy of free love. While for the old anarchists "free love" had meant heterosexual companionship free of the sanction of church or state, it was updated in the 1960s to signify unrepressed sexuality unconstrained by conventional mores. Overall, the practices of the New Left and the counterculture resembled anarchist ideals much more than communist ones. Everywhere communes, collectives, back-to-nature movements proliferated; urban, technological society was rejected as alienating and impersonal, and an intense demand for community and solidarity as well as for individuality and personal freedom manifested itself among the young. These new utopians rejected the work ethic, the hierarchies of corporation and university, the patriarchal nuclear family, and rampant consumerism as much as they protested against class- and race-based oppression. In other words, the familiar anarchist criticism of domination figured as largely in their rhetoric as did the Marxist language of exploitation. Politics was not conceived of as an impersonal force located in classes or races, nor was it confined to elections or even to revolutionary struggles; politics was perceived as pervading everyday life. Students demanded relevance and immediacy; the personal was political.

Just as anarchism has always tended toward a wide-ranging critique of the dominant ethos, so the countercultural movement of the 1960s sought to replace a society based on perceived domination, hierarchy, and impersonal scientific rationality with one based on such values as spontaneity, intuition, community—in short, on "love." Yet the 1960s were marked not only by love but also by violent confrontations between increasingly defensive governments and militant protesters, and here too the anarchist conflict between utopian goals and violent tactics emerged. All the talk of revolution combined with values celebrating direct action led to open conflict, and even to terrorism by a relatively few alienated groups. However, the American terrorist Weatherman faction of SDS, the Red Brigade of Italy, and the Baader-Meinhof gang of West Germany all considered themselves to be Marxists rather than anarchists. Modern anarchists seem to have outgrown terrorism, and favored instead the options of either promoting spontaneous insurrection or preserving their distance from the mainstream in communes that would exemplify anarchist values. The anarchist ideal of revolution found its nearest equivalent in the May 1968 events in France.

If most young American activists were at all aware of the traditions of the left, they were liable to refer indiscriminately to Marx and Bakunin, whereas the French New Left was more historically conscious. Thus Daniel Cohn-Bendit, who achieved celebrity in the minirevolution of May 1968, placed himself squarely in the tradition of the Paris Commune, and in his book *Obsolete Communism: The Left-Wing Alternative* he referred back to Nestor Makhno in the Ukraine and to the Kronstadt uprising against the Bolshevik party in 1921, both of which were largely anarchist movements. Just as Emma Goldman attacked the Bolsheviks for perverting the Russian Revolution of 1917 and George Orwell condemned the Communist party for wrecking the Spanish Revolution of 1936, so Cohn-Bendit stigmatized the French Communist party in 1968 as a force of the "bureaucratic counter-revolution."[5] The trade union leadership of the Confédération Générale du Travail (CGT), which at its inception has been anarcho-syndicalist, dragged its feet as the revolutionary ferment spread from the students to the workers, yet at one point ten million French workers joined the students in a spontaneous general strike that almost toppled the government of Charles de Gaulle.

The revolution of May 1968 originated earlier that spring in student demands for education reforms. Throughout Europe the college population had expanded far faster than institutions had. In the overcrowded lecture halls professors still read their lectures formally to students who craved more involvement in their education. Protests began at the raw, new campus of Nanterre on the outskirts of Paris, where Cohn-Bendit, a German exchange student, led sit-ins demanding more student control over their education. Whether a slogan demanded student, black, gay, or women's power, everywhere people were seeking greater control over their own lives. The French students were not satisfied with the reforms issuing from ministries in the highly centralized French government; instead they demanded continuing input into the nature of those changes. They sought no particular reforms, but rather the abolition of hierarchical authority. Their means were acts of civil disobedience. When government forces overreacted and wounded many students at the Sorbonne in May, the confrontation escalated and the students were further radicalized. They "liberated" their campuses and scrawled slogans on the walls that encapsulated the spirit of '68:

> It is forbidden to forbid. Freedom begins by a prohibition: that of hurting the freedom of others.
>
> A cop sleeps in every one of us, he must be killed.
>
> There is no revolutionary thought. There are only revolutionary acts.
>
> Anarchy is I.[6]

In the conclusion of his book about that year, Cohn-Bendit underscored the anarchistic spirit of ongoing revolt that was captured in the graffiti of Paris: "If a revolutionary movement is to succeed, no form of organization whatever must be allowed to dam its spontaneous flow. It must evolve its own forms and structures." Then he listed some central issues that all future movements must pursue. These included resistance against any kind of hierarchy; abolition of all "artificial distinctions within labor, in particular between manual and intellectual work, and discrimination on grounds of sex," the guarantee that "all factories and businesses are run by those who work in them"; and even the end of the Judeo-Christian ethic of renunciation and sacrifice. He concluded that "there is only one reason for being a revolutionary—because it is the best way to live."[7] Means and ends finally collapsed; revolution became a way of life.

The French government did not collapse under the student onslaught; in fact in the elections called the following month, the Gaullists profited from a backlash against student disorder and made their greatest showing ever at the polls. The liberal intellectual Raymond Aron lambasted students for engaging in mere revolutionary psychodrama. There was indeed a self-dramatizing quality to this revolution called by relatively privileged members of society.

Beyond such ideological goals as an end to Western imperialism lay a more personal quest for authentic experience. The experience of utopia—a profound break with ordinary time and space and a sense of transcending the mundane present—justified revolution as an end in itself. The "sixty-eighters," as these students have been identified ever since, experienced the same feelings of euphoric exaltation as did the Communards of 1871 or the anarchists of Barcelona in 1936, and this reinforced their sense of separateness from the dominant society.

Only a small minority of the activists of the 1960s consciously identified themselves with the anarchist tradition. Partly out of political naïveté, partly out of a distrust for labels and ideologies inherited from a distant and proletarian past, the New Left remained ideologically amorphous. If not explicitly libertarian (a term that was problematic anyway in the American context, having been appropriated by proponents of laissez-faire capitalism and minimal government), the student activists did favor "liberation" in a variety of guises, from the liberation of the peasants of Vietnam to the freeing of one's body from a society practicing "repressive sublimation." This latter phrase came from one of the most influential New Left theorists, Herbert Marcuse, who came not out of the anarchist but the neo-Marxist tradition of the Frankfurt School for Social Research. The Frankfurt School had deviated from Marxist orthodoxy in the 1920s and after in its emphasis on issues pertaining to culture and mass consumption rather than class. Marcuse, Erich Fromm, and Wilhelm Reich all attempted to graft a Marxist theory of exploitation onto a Freudian understanding of psychic repression, to demonstrate the personally deadening effect of modern capitalist society. This concern for the psychic integrity of the individual had always been lacking among the overly class-oriented socialists, and it coincided neatly with the anarchists' valuation of personal autonomy. If the difference between Marxists and anarchists was that the former sought freedom through equality and the latter equality through freedom, then this neo-Marxism of the New Left seemed closer to the latter. For all of the dispossessed and alienated groups demanding social change, the clarion call was "Freedom now!"

Anarcha-Feminism

One of the chief results of the emphasis on the personal dimension of politics was that people were encouraged to explore the ways in which power relations affected their own lives. One of the most important movements to develop out of this sixties matrix was that of women's liberation. After the first wave of feminism peaked shortly after World War I with the granting of women's suffrage in most Western countries, women were relatively quiescent, especially in the two decades after the Second World War, when they were enjoined to take their place at the center of the nuclear family. In the postwar baby boom, women of the rapidly expanding middle class were kept busy having and raising children. But those children—the baby-boomers—grew up to question the value of endless mass consumption made possible by relatively affluent societies, and the women of that new generation questioned in particular the role of women in the family and in society. The radicalism of the sixties led directly to the radical feminism of the late sixties and after.

If *radical* can mean getting to the root of the problem, for the radical feminists, that fundamental problem was patriarchy. The division of the world into male-dominated warring polities was mirrored on the social level by male authority in the family, as exercised by husbands and fathers. Self-styled sixties "Anarcha-feminists" spoke of "gangs of armed males calling themselves governments," and demanded an end to the twin bastions of male authority.[8] They perceived radical feminism as being inherently anarchistic, insofar as it identified the climate of authority ensconced in family and state as the source not only of women's oppression but also of the aggression rampant in the modern world.

The spontaneous development of women's collectives and consciousness-raising groups in the late sixties and seventies was likened to the anarchist affinity groups of earlier times. These feminist groups extended traditional anarchist hostility toward religion to include criticism of the patriarchal nature of the Judeo-Christian tradition, which they implicated in the exploitation not only of women but also of nature, indeed of the entire external world.[9] Men objectified nature and the Other, the better to dominate them; women, they argued, were more capable of subject-to-subject relationships. The anarcha-feminist critique of male power was even extended to the anarchist movement itself, which despite its libertarian ideals had failed to abolish the subjection of women, even among radicals. Feminism was perceived to be as vital to anarchism as anarchism was to feminism.[10] In the United States, interest in the life and career of Emma Goldman, who had actively supported birth control and sexual freedom in the great anarchist heyday before the

First World War, revived in the sixties. Young people sported T-shirts inscribed with a slogan attributed to "Red Emma": "If I can't dance, I don't want your revolution."

Murray Bookchin and the Ecological Perspective

Radical feminists have linked the subordination of women to the exploitation of nature, and one would expect the liberation of one to imply a reevaluation of the other. Indeed, the most important new focus besides the women's movement to emerge in the 1960s and 1970s concerned attitudes toward nature. People began to reassess the costs of the industrial revolution, which had utterly transformed the planet in less than two hundred years. One cannot claim that anarchism was central to the emerging ecology movement, yet it dovetailed perfectly with a radical interpretation of the root causes of the environmental problems afflicting the planet.

In this, anarchism had a tremendous advantage over Marxism, which was locked into a nineteenth-century productivist ethic. Anarchists, historically, were sensitive to the antiprogressive biases of peasants and artisans, while Marx for the most part had viewed technology as being ideologically neutral. What mattered was who controlled the means of production, not the means themselves. His disciple, Lenin, had famously defined communism as the soviet plus electrification. Soon thereafter, in Russia and elsewhere, centralized communism largely functioned to plan economic development in Third World countries. Trotsky said it succinctly: "The very purpose of communism is to subject nature to technique and technique to plan, and compel the raw materials to give . . . everything to man that he needs."[11] The environmental consequences of this productivist ethic became clear with the end of communism in eastern Europe; communism was worse, ecologically, than capitalism. If Marxism had been an appropriate ideology for the age of the industrial revolution, perhaps anarchism would be better suited for dealing with the problems of a postindustrial world.

This last point is ironic, given the Marxists' tendency to classify anarchism as a primitive and irrational movement that had faded out along with its peasant and artisan constituency. Anarchism's modern incarnation has been advanced principally by the contemporary American anarchist philosopher Murray Bookchin, who, in several books published in the past thirty years, has done more than anyone else to redefine the relevance of anarchism for our times. Bookchin is a technological modernist who argues that the basis for the anarchist utopia finally exists in our "post-scarcity" economy. The highly centralized state, large-scale industry, and exclusively working-class focus of Marxism are all obsolete; instead he argues that we need to achieve a human-scale society and economy based on values of variety, diversity, locality, and balance. Bookchin follows Kropotkin in rooting anarchist values scientifically. While physics and astronomy were the cutting-edge sciences of the early modern era and biology was central to the nineteenth century, Bookchin sees ecology as the most progressive scientific approach of the twentieth century. He argues that anarchist ideas that were dismissed as visionary a century ago are today not only practical but also necessary to save our planet from ourselves. He finds these values so congruent with those of the science of ecology that he uses the term *social ecology* as a synonym for anarchism, which has the double benefit of replacing a negative ("without rulers") term drawn from political philosophy with a positive one drawn from science.

Bookchin advanced these ideas as early as 1971 in his book *Post-Scarcity Anarchism*, but he did not work them out fully until a decade later, when he published his magnum opus, *The Ecology of Freedom: The Emergence and Dissolution of Hierarchy*. Between these two important books he also wrote a history of Spanish anarchism and another on modern urbanism. The most important anarchist thinker since Kropotkin, Bookchin resembles his great predecessor not only in his scientific orientation but also in the remarkable range of his thought. In his synthesizing of history, philosophy, ecology, anthropology, and sociology into a coherent approach he reminds one of Marx as well, and in fact Bookchin began his intellectual life as a Marxist of Trotskyist persuasion. (Born in 1921, Bookchin became an anarchist in the 1950s). He freely acknowledges his intellectual debt to the unorthodox Marxists of the Frankfurt School, and remains in some ways Hegelian in his thinking (freedom is "uninhibited volition and self-consciousness";[12] truth, the self-consummation of a process through its immanent development.)

Yet Bookchin's attack on the dominant tendencies of Marxism is devastating: he claims that Marx and Engels made a fetish of the working class, at a time when industrial authority was rendering workers increasingly passive. If the proletariat was not at the forefront of protest then, he argues, it certainly is not now, and anarchists must look to new groups and issues. Communism is no different than capitalism in its devotion to instrumental rationality. What Bookchin calls authoritarian reason is oriented toward control, manipulation, domination, and estrangement; libertarian reason, on the other hand, is ecologically symbiotic, nurturing, and deobjectifying.[13] Marxism was devoted to objectifying and dominating the masses, anarchism to liberating the subjective individual.

In maintaining that ecology is a potentially radicalizing science, Bookchin is careful to distinguish it from mere environmentalism, which is easily assimilated by liberal reformists who accept humans' domination of nature but wish to reduce its costs. An ecological perspective always implies awareness of the whole, of complex patterns of relationship, which Bookchin describes as forming a unity in diversity. Such an interdependent whole is dynamic rather than static, and above all, he claims, antihierarchical. This is the crux of his argument linking ecology and anarchy: In a truly interdependent ecosystem, no part of it can dominate without upsetting the balance. "To rank species within an ecosystem, that is to say, between species, is anthropomorphism at its crudest."[14] Ecological awareness is meant to revivify social awareness, to act as a metaphor for the kind of society that Bookchin would like to see: democratic, decentralized, nonexploitive, human-scaled. This society would maximize freedom, pleasure, and self-expression rather than production. But of course ecology is not simply a metaphor, for Bookchin believes that only a "social ecological" society can preserve the ecology of the planet and thus human as well as other life in the biosphere.

Such a recasting of anarchism is light-years away from anarcho-syndicalist talk of general strikes and seizures of factories. Its postindustrial, postnationalist, world-community orientation makes it a compelling vision of the future. It updates Kropotkin's optimistic belief that mankind is evolving toward anarchy as a superior form of organization that is somehow naturally immanent. As Kropotkin did, Bookchin idealizes medieval life, not only for its autonomous communes and communal social matrix but also for its use of windmills and waterwheels as power sources that minimized environmental degradation. Like Kropotkin and Landauer, he bemoans the shift that took place around the time of Francis Bacon, from organic to mechanistic epistemologies that sanctioned exploitation of nature and idealized power and control. Bookchin's thought is itself holistic in interrelating history, politics, economics, and ecology—the better to demonstrate that human freedom and progress depend on human beings' complementarity with, not subjection of, nature. Kropotkin, Landauer, and Bookchin would welcome the end of the five-hundred-year era of Western dynamism, to be replaced by a more balanced and truly conservative society dedicated to preserving human and natural values. Yet as we have seen, their ideas of freedom were developed at the high point of the Enlightenment's celebration of human reason and progress.

Radical Ecologists

Bookchin's work has not provided the sort of theoretical underpinnings for the radical ecology movement that one might have expected. His work might remind one of the European Green Movement, which makes similar connections between antimilitarism, feminism, and antinuclear activism within an overall ecological perspective. The Green movement definitely stemmed from the 1960s and saw itself as transcending the Cold War confrontation between East and West with a new constellation of issues. But their electoral orientation—the German Green party held a considerable number of seats in the West German Bundestag in the 1980s—distances the Greens from anarchism, however unconventional their politics may be.

Even closer to anarchism, especially in their direct-action tactics, is the American radical ecology group Earth First!, which is dedicated to resisting development projects that it believes threaten the remaining natural environment in the American West. Unlike the mainline environmental public interest groups, Earth First! engages in a kind of industrial sabotage, called monkeywrenching, that involves such acts as pouring sand into the gas tanks of bulldozers at construction sites, or pounding iron spikes into trees to prevent their being cut by timber companies (a process that does not harm the tree but makes it commercially unusable, and that also presents hazards to the lumber company employee operating the chainsaw). Earth First! founder Dave Foreman believes that all species have an equal right to inhabit the planet, and that human beings have vastly overpopulated the earth. They are therefore radically antinatal, and they also seek to stop immigration into the United States, with the goal of reducing the U.S. population to a level that would permit the preservation of much greater areas of wilderness.

Though Earth First! members are directly inspired by anarchism, their mentor is not Murray Bookchin, whose very name resonates with New York Jewish intellectuality; he is the western American novelist and essayist Edward Abbey, who died in 1989 at the age of 62. Abbey contributed the foreword to Foreman's book *Ecodefense: A Field Guide to Monkeywrenching* (published by Ned Ludd Books), as he had earlier bequeathed a name to the tactic in his novel *The Monkey Wrench Gang,* published in 1975.

Abbey's love of the wide open spaces of the American West led him to equate the West with freedom in a typically American way. But even though his novels were liable to enshrine the cowboy as the emblem of individualism, his heart was really closer to the Native Americans, whose hunting-and-gathering way of life required a degree of intimacy with their environment that the white man, always just passing through, hardly glimpsed. Abbey brought a misanthropic tone to anarchism that was largely missing from the European and eastern American orientation, based on the feeling that humans must leave their fellow humans and the artifacts of culture behind and make contact with nature in its most primordial state if they wish to achieve self-knowledge. Abbey hearkened back to Henry David Thoreau, who left Boston society to commune with nature at Walden Pond, and whose epigram, "In wildness is the preservation of the world," made its way onto countless students' dormitory walls in the 1960s and 1970s. Such was Abbey's disgust at what American industrial culture had wrought that he came to identify freedom and authenticity with a natural world in which all traces of humanity were expunged. His intensely individualistic anarchism was a long way from Kropotkin's idealization of the social world of the medieval commune, as Abbey's deep distrust of technology diverged from Kropotkin's optimism about scientific progress.

A good example of Abbey's work is contained in the essay "Down the River with Henry Thoreau," in which he described how he left civilization on 4 November 1980 to take a ten-day raft trip down the Green River, so as to enjoy the landscape of southeastern Utah and to remain in temporary blissful ignorance of the presidential election held on that day. He commented on bumper stickers he had seen during the Carter-Reagan campaign—"Question Authority" and "Nobody for President"—and quoted Thoreau's statement "that government is best which governs not at all." He then editorialized,

Year by year the institutions that dominate our lives grow even bigger, more complicated, massive, impersonal, and powerful. Whether governmental, corporate, military, or technological—and how can any one of these be disentangled from the others?—they weigh on society as the pyramids of Egypt weighed on the backs of those who were conscripted to build them. The pyramids of power. Five thousand years later the people of Egypt still have not recovered. They remain a passive, debased mass of subjects. Mere fellahin, expendable and interchangeable units in a social megamachine. As if the pride and spirit had been crushed from them forever.[15]

When Abbey contrasted his trip down the Green River with the rat race that most people led—leading lives of quiet desperation, as Thoreau put it—he was echoing the anarchist-naturalist tradition of Kropotkin, Landauer, and Bookchin. Yet radical ecologists criticize the implicit humanism of this tradition as being overly anthropocentric. Attaining a nonhierarchical balance with nature means removing humankind from its privileged position, which in turn implies greatly decreasing our exploitation of the resources of the planet for our material benefit. Abbey's mental landscape of austere harmony would seem to return "postscarcity" society to the antimaterialist vision of the *obreros conscientes* of anarchist Spain, who regarded the bourgeoisie as unduly luxurious and corrupt—as decadent. Edward Abbey and the entire naturalist school of anarchists are undoubtedly moralists in this sense, condemning a way of life that has substituted material wealth for freedom and authenticity. Anarchists are cultural revolutionaries to a much greater degree than Marxists can be, tied as they are to a materialist, class analysis of revolution.

The transition from anarchy to ecology has not been quite as smooth as the foregoing discussion might indicate. At the end of the 1980s, Murray Bookchin lashed out at the movement he referred to as "deep ecology," in contrast to his theory of social ecology, and singled out Earth First! for a special attack. He called Dave Foreman an "eco-brutalist" and a misanthropic mountain man who advocated letting the Ethiopian people starve so as to render their country more ecologically viable. He referred to a notorious Earth First! newspaper editorial, which had calmly accepted the AIDS virus as a natural control mechanism that would help "correct" human overpopulation, as an example of vicious Malthusianism. Bookchin was disturbed by many ecologists' tendency to stigmatize humanity in general rather than capitalism, and the privileged classes, and countries or governments in particular. He was absolutely incensed by the "New Age" spirituality of the 1980s that had led to nature-worship, witchcraft, and a general cult of the primal. In his most outrageous statement in an intemperate article, Bookchin wrote that "the Paleolithic shaman in reindeer skin and horns is the predecessor of the Pharaoh and the Buddha and, in more recent times, of Hitler, Stalin and Mussolini."[15] He took the rationalist high ground against blood-and-soil mystagogy, which he felt smacked of fascist irrationalism. This was clearly excessive; "social" and "deep" ecology are far more alike than they are different. Whether Bookchin was piqued at not being considered the father of the ecology movement or whether he sincerely felt that the radical ecologists' biotic focus impeded their social and economic analysis of the causes of environmental degradation, he produced the sort of internecine feuding that too often has plagued the left.

From Situationists to Punks

The anarchist demand for "direct action" has usually been taken to imply violence, but direct action has a spiritual meaning, too. From Proudhon's idealization of the artisan's workshop to Abbey's equation of virtue with finding oneself through immersion in the wilderness, anarchists have championed the immediacy of experience. They have disliked delegating authority to others; power is a zero-sum game, they believe, so power bequeathed to others is no longer available to you. Anarchists would likewise condemn our mediated society, which increasingly replaces direct with vicarious experience, life with an image of life. People consume not only things but also images; advertising agencies commodify presidential candidates as readily as processed cheese spread. The price of substituting manufactured desires for our real ones is passivity, alienation, and "unfreedom," as people live chained to their credit cards in pursuit of some ideal images of themselves.

The criticism that modern society is fundamentally a spectacle, defined not as a "collection of images, but a social relation among people, mediated by images," was made most cogently by a group of French intellectuals who called themselves the Situationist International (SI). A journal by that name existed from 1958 until 1969, edited by Guy Debord, who also published *Society of the Spectacle* a year before Paris exploded in the events of May 1968. The clashes of 1968 gave the clique some notoriety as the conspiracy behind the insurrection, and SI slogans such as "I take my desires for reality because I believe in the reality of my desires" appeared on Parisian walls.[17] Like others on the New Left, SI focused on the domination and banality inherent in everyday life. They extended Marx's early perception that bourgeois society had substituted "having" for "being" by noting that mass-consumption society had replaced "having" with "appearing." Debord's language is reminiscent of that of Theodor Adorno and other Frankfurt School theorists, and therefore had only limited popular appeal. If not strictly anarchist, the brunt of his message was certainly within the libertarian tradition: "The oldest social specialization, the specialization of power, is at the root of the spectacle. . . . It is the diplomatic representation of hierarchic society to itself. . . . The spectacle is the existing order's uninterrupted discourse about itself, its laudatory monologue. It is the self-portrait of power in the epoch of its totalitarian management of the conditions of existence."[18] The cover of the American edition of Debord's book shows a movie theater crowd all wearing identical eyeglasses (spectacles) designed for watching three-dimensional films, giving them a mesmerized, zombielike appearance.

The Situationists wanted to create revolutionary events that would dramatize the absurdity of contemporary life and their alienation from it, and that would negate the spectacle. Their ultimate situation was the May Revolution of 1968, which they partly influenced. They linked up with a group called the Enragés, after Jacques Roux's ultrarevolutionary movement of 1793. As false existence was stripped away, real communication and self-expression became possible, and the personal and the social-historical realms merged. The new French revolutionaries dramatized their libertarian aspirations by such means as the following telegram sent by the Enragés/SI to the Politburo of the Communist party in Moscow:

SHAKE IN YOUR SHOES BUREAUCRATS STOP THE
INTERNATIONAL POWER OF THE WORKERS COUN-
CILS WILL SOON WIPE YOU OUT STOP HUMANITY
WILL NOT BE HAPPY UNTIL THE LAST BUREAUCRAT
IS HUNG WITH THE GUTS OF THE LAST CAPITALIST
STOP LONG LIVE THE STRUGGLE OF THE KRONSTADT
SAILORS AND OF THE MAKNOVSCHINA AGAINST

TROTSKY AND LENIN STOP LONG LIVE THE 1956 COUNCILIST INSURRECTION OF BUDAPEST STOP DOWN WITH THE STATE[19]

There is no record of a reply to this anarchist provocation, which was issued from the Sorbonne, indicating that the Parisian students saw other precedents besides the Paris Commune. Unfortunately these precedents were generally as ephemeral as the students' own occupation of the university would be. (Makhno's Ukrainian anarchist regime was the only one to last more than a few weeks or months.)

In his provocative book *Lipstick Traces*, Greil Marcus links the Situationists with other twentieth-century radical culture negators. He sees a "secret history" extending from the dadaists of the World War I era to the punk rock movement of the mid to late 1970s; from Hugo Ball's performances at the Cabaret Voltaire in Zurich in 1916 to the Situationists' carnivalization of Paris in 1968 to the punk group the Sex Pistol's pleas for "Anarchy in the U.K." in 1975. Marcus experienced a similar cultural-historical moment of his own during the Free Speech movement at the University of California at Berkeley in 1964. During these moments, Marcus writes, revolution seems imminent, liberation of self and society at hand. The moment inevitably fades but the memory remains, and one is never quite the same again.[20]

What Marcus seems to be describing is the revolutionary ecstasy characteristic of chiliastic movements, a quasireligious belief that the millennium is at hand, that the world is liable to change totally at any moment, that the New Jerusalem is here and now. The German sociologist Karl Mannheim called this sense of time "absolute presentness," and believed it characterized both traditional millenarian movements and modern-day anarchism.[21] As rooted as anarchist thought has been in Enlightenment rationality, it would seem that the experience of revolution precedes the Age of Reason. One can find its origins among the Levelers and Diggers of the English civil war or the Anabaptists of the Reformation or among medieval heretics; all were religious revolutionaries. The Sex Pistols rhymed "anarchist" with "antichrist" to emphasize their heretical stance. "Direct action" has its experiential, revolutionary counterpart in absolute presentness, the exaltation derived from the feeling that one's person is merged with the body politic, a state that effaces the perennial anarchist conflict between individual freedom and social solidarity. To acknowledge this spirit is not to "put down" the anarchists as prepolitical primitives, but rather to recognize the nonrational aspects of both revolution and history. Beneath the "cunning of reason" lies divine madness when personal and social liberation coincide.

Conclusion

The phrase "lipstick traces" is meant to evoke the ephemeral nature of much of the twentieth century avant-garde. Surely that description is not appropriate for the larger anarchist movement recorded in these pages, yet the question remains: Is anarchism confined to historical memory, or does it retain a continuing relevance for our times? Historians are justifiably uncomfortable when asked to predict the future, but at least one can say that the profound political transformations of the late 1980s and early 1990s make it premature to write off anarchism.

In 1989, Czechoslovakia and East Germany witnessed genuinely spontaneous revolutions. The revolutions of 1989 in Eastern Europe were started by a politically radical workers' union in Poland (though in this case, the Solidarity union was opposing a communist, not a capitalist, state). Socialists have liked to say that the general strike is general nonsense, yet the communist government of Albania was brought down by such a strike in 1991; the new president agreed to all the workers' demands, including a 50 percent pay raise. And in Moscow, when the ex-communist president of Russia, Boris Yeltsin, mounted a tank to oppose the communist coup on 19 August 1991, he called for a general strike throughout the Soviet Union.

As communism collapsed, so did the centralized state it had enforced. Federalism or outright secession has become the order of the day in the Soviet Union and Yugoslavia. Certainly ethnic rivalries and identities are crucial to this decentralist movement, and yet throughout Europe, both east and west, the centralized nation-state that reigned supreme a century ago is becoming increasingly irrelevant. On the one hand, regionalism asserts itself in Catalonia and the Basque country of Spain, in Wales and Scotland in Great Britain, and elsewhere; on the other, the new European Community is effacing national borders.

As the center falls apart, this does not necessarily signify that anarchy is being loosed upon the world; after all, the former leader of Solidarity is now chief of state in Poland, and everywhere people seem to be clamoring for entry into the market economy. So great is the disillusionment with communism that there do not seem to be calls for council communism to replace the party variety.[22] Still, the decline of Marxism would seem, at the least, to warrant paying closer attention to the anarchist analysis of revolution and human needs.[23] If the social-ecological perspective of Murray Bookchin becomes better known, as the world's environment continues to degrade, there may come a time when people will want to know more about the much-abused movement called anarchism. Or perhaps it will go by an entirely different name, shorn of the associations with negativism and violence that have hampered anarchism's spread. If the core ideas of freedom, decentralization, and direct democracy remain, I suspect that a rebirth under a different aegis would please Proudhon, Kropotkin, Goldman, and the rest of the band of activists and ideologues who shook the world in pursuit of their dream.

Chronology

1756   William Godwin born.

1793   Godwin's *Enquiry Concerning Political Justice* published.
        Radical Jacobin phase of French Revolution.

1806   Max Stirner (Johann Caspar Schmidt) born.

1809   Pierre-Joseph Proudhon born.

1814   Mikhail Bakunin born.

1818   Karl Marx born.

1836   Godwin dies.

1840   Proudhon's *What Is Property?* published.
        Bakunin leaves Russia for Germany.

1842   Peter Kropotkin born.

1844   Stirner's *The Ego and Its Own* published.

1846   Proudhon's *System of Economic Contradictions, or The Philosophy of Poverty* published.

1847   Marx attacks Proudhon in *The Poverty of Philosophy.*

1848   Revolutions break out all over Europe. Proudhon elected to French National Assembly.
        Marx and Engel's *Communist Manifesto* published.

1849   Proudhon sent to prison for three years for criticizing President Louis Napoleon.

Bakunin fights on barricades in Dresden, Saxony. He is arrested, condemned to death, then handed over to Austrians, then to Russians.

1851 Bakunin, imprisoned in Russia until 1857, writes *Confession to the Czar.*

1858 Proudhon's *Of Justice in the Revolution and in the Church* published. Exiled in Belgium until 1862.

1861 Bakunin escapes from Siberian exile.

1863 Proudhon's *The Principle of Federation* published.

1864 Marx founds International Working Men's Association (IWMA) in London.
Bakunin founds International Brotherhood in Italy.

1865 Proudhon dies.

1868 Bakunin founds International Alliance for Social Democracy.
In Spain, Queen Isabella overthrown; Giuseppe Fanelli arrives, founds branch of Bakunin's International Alliance.

1869 Bakunin meets Sergei Nechaev; they write *Revolutionary Catechism.*

1870 Gustav Landauer born.
Franco-Prussian War begins.

1871 Paris Commune, 18 March to 28 May.

1872 IWMA meets in The Hague, votes to move General Council to New York to be safe from Bakuninist influence. Bakunin expelled for maintaining separate, secret organization.

1874 Bakunin participates in attempted insurrection in Bologna.

1876 Bakunin dies.
Kropotkin escapes from Russian prison.

1877 Errico Malatesta and Carlo Cafiero attempt uprising in Benevento, Italy.

1879 Kropotkin founds journal *Le Révolté* in Switzerland.

1881 Czar Alexander II assassinated by Russian populists.
Anarchists hold international congress in London.

1882   Bakunin's *God and the State* published, edited by Elisée
       Reclus and Cafiero.

1883   Marx dies.
       Kropotkin imprisoned in France for three years.

1885   Jean Grave moves *Le Révolté* to Paris, changes name to
       La Révolte.

1886   Bomb thrown in Haymarket Square, Chicago, 4 May.
       Four anarchists hanged in Chicago, 11 November. Trial
       and execution give anarchists massive propaganda.
       Journal *Freedom* founded in London.

1889   Second Socialist International founded in Paris.
       Anarchists denied entry; meet separately.

1890   May Day celebrated as workers' holiday.

1891   May Day demonstrators fired on at Fourmies, France.
       Anarchism attains growing literary following.

1892   Advent of widespread terrorist activities. In United
       States, Alexander Berkman tries to assassinate Carnegie
       Steel manager Henry Clay Frick in Pennsylvania.
       In Paris, François Ravachol places bombs at homes of
       judge and prosecutor; during his trial, bomb kills
       proprietor of restaurant who informed on him.
       In Jerez, Spain, abortive uprising leads to many
       executions.
       Kropotkin's *The Conquest of Bread* published.

1893   Further bombings: Santiago Salvador kills twenty
       people in Liceo Theater in Barcelona, leading to much
       repression and many executions. Auguste Vaillant
       throws bomb into French Chamber of Deputies. No one
       is killed, but legislature passes stiff laws limiting
       freedom of press.

1894   Émile Henry throws bomb at Café Terminus at Gare St.
       Lazare in Paris.
       French president Sadi Carnot killed in Lyon.
       Intellectuals acquitted in French Trial of Thirty.

1895   Fernand Pelloutier becomes general secretary of
       Fédération des Bourses du Travail.
       Confédération Générale du Travail (CGT) founded,
       anarcho-syndicalism born.

1896   Corpus Christi Day bombing in Barcelona leads to further repression.

1897   Premier Cánovas of Spain assassinated.

1898   Empress Elizabeth of Austria assassinated.

1899   Kropotkin's *Memoirs of a Revolutionist* published.

1900   King Umberto I of Italy assassinated.

1901   U.S. president William McKinley assassinated.

1902   Bourses du Travail and CGT combine.
Kropotkin's *Mutual Aid* published.

1903   U.S. Congress passes law barring entry of anarchist aliens.

1905   Industrial Workers of the World (IWW) founded in United States.

1906   CGT Congress of Amiens reaffirms anarcho-syndicalist principles, including freedom from all political influence.
Georges Sorel's *Reflections on Violence* published.

1907   International anarchist congress at Amsterdam; Pierre Monatte and Malatesta debate on relation of anarchism and syndicalism.

1908   Landauer's *The Revolution* published.

1909   Barcelona errupts in riots in July: La Semana Tragica. Authorities seize Francisco Ferrer, founder of Modern School, and execute him for alleged participation.

1910   Confederación Nacional de Trabajo (CNT) founded in Spain.
Sidney Street Affair, London.

1912   IWW strike in Lawrence, Massachusetts.

1914   Red Week riots and general strike in Italy in June.
World War I splits anarchists, with Kropotkin and Grave siding with France against Germany, despite long antimilitarism.

1917   Russian Revolution; Kropotkin returns to Russia but loses following when he supports Alexander Kerensky in continuing war effort.
Nestor Makhno gains anarchist influence in Ukraine.

1918–20	Russian civil war; anarchists under Makhno spar with Austrians, Ukrainian nationalists, Reds, and Whites.
1919	Wave of bombings in United States. Berkman, Emma Goldman, and other U.S. anarchists deported. Landauer murdered in Munich.
1921	Kropotkin dies. His funeral is occasion of the last anarchist demonstration in Russia. Makhno goes into exile. Kronstadt naval uprising put down by Trotsky. Goldman and Berkman leave Russia for Western Europe. Nicola Sacco and Bartolomeo Vanzetti condemned to death for murder-robbery in Massachusetts.
1922	International Working Men's Association founded in Berlin.
1923	Salvador Segui killed in wave of violence in Spain.
1924	General Primo de Rivera declares CNT illegal.
1927	Federación Anarquista Ibérica (FAI) founded. Sacco and Vanzetti executed, amid worldwide protests.
1931	Collapse of Spanish monarchy, advent of Second Republic.
1932	Malatesta dies.
1933	Anarchist uprisings in Spain; massacre at Casas Viejas.
1934	Miners of Asturias revolt.
1936	Berkman commits suicide. Right-wing revolt against Second Republic begins Spanish civil war, with anarchists playing major role in defending the republic and creating social revolution. Goldman comes to Spain to lend her support. Buenaventura Durruti dies in defense of Madrid. Four anarchists take ministerial portfolios in Largo Caballero's government.
1937	Communists defeat anarchists in Barcelona in May.
1939	General Francisco Franco defeats loyalists with help from Hitler and Mussolini. Anarchists stream across Pyrenees into exile.

1940 Goldman dies.

1954 Herbert Read's *Anarchy and Order* published.

1957 Situationist International founded in Paris.

1960 Paul Goodman's *Growing Up Absurd*, and A. S. Neill's *Summerhill* published.

1962 George Woodcock's *Anarchism* published.

1967 Guy Debord's *Society of the Spectacle* published.

1968 May Events in Paris, student takeover of Sorbonne and general strike paralyzing France. Daniel Cohn-Bendit's *Obsolete Communism* published.
Yippies mock Democratic party convention in Chicago, provoking police riot.
Socialist humanism crushed in Czechoslovakia.

1968–70 Widespread civil disobedience, antidraft protests in United States. Upsurge of interest in anarchism.

1971 Murray Bookchin's *Post-Scarcity Anarchism* published.

1975 Edward Abbey's *The Monkey Wrench Gang* published.

1982 Bookchin's *Ecology of Freedom* published.

1989 Collapse of communism in Eastern Europe.

1991 Collapse of communism in the Soviet Union, disintegration of the central government.

Notes and References

1. THE PLACE OF ANARCHISM

1. The novels in question are James's *The Princess Casamassima* (1885), Zola's *Paris* (1898), Conrad's *The Secret Agent* (1908), and Chesterton's *The Man Who Was Thursday* (1908).

2. Paul Avrich, *Sacco and Vanzetti: The Anarchist Background* (Princeton: Princeton University Press, 1991), 162. Avrich calls their participation in the bombings of 1919 a "virtual certainty." See pp. 205, 206 for the Wall Street bombing.

2. THE PHILOSOPHY OF ANARCHISM

1. James Joll, *The Anarchists* 2d ed. (Cambridge, Mass.: Harvard University Press, 1980), 16.

2. Godwin thus takes his place in the Manuels' magisterial tour of utopian thought. See Frank E. Manuel and Fritzie P. Manuel, *Utopian Thought in the Western World* (Cambridge, Mass.: Harvard University Press, 1979), 735, 736. See also Joll, *The Anarchists*, 16–24.

3. R. W. K. Paterson, The Nihilistic Egoist: Max Stirner (New York: Oxford University Press, 1971), 22–25.

4. Paterson, *The Nihilistic Egoist*, 3–6.

5. John Carroll, *Break-Out from the Crystal Palace, The Anarcho-Psychological Critique: Stirner, Nietzsche, Dostoevsky* (London: Routledge and Kegan Paul, 1974), 15.

6. Paterson, *The Nihilistic Egoist*, 62–64.

7. Paterson, *The Nihilistic Egoist*, 65, 66.

8. Paterson, *The Nihilistic Egoist*, 109–111.

9. Paterson, *The Nihilistic Egoist*, 81.

10. Eugene Lunn, *Prophet of Community: The Mystical Anarchism of Gustav Landauer* (Berkeley: University of California Press, 1973), 106.

11. For this and the following information concerning Rousseau and Proudhon, see Aaron Noland, "Proudhon and Rousseau," *Journal of the History of Ideas* 28, no. 1 (1967): 33–54.

12. Paul Thomas, *Karl Marx and the Anarchists* (London: Routledge and Kegan Paul, 1980), 10.

13. George Woodcock, *Pierre-Joseph Proudhon* (New York: Macmillan, 1956), 73.

14. Robert L. Hoffman, *Revolutionary Justice: The Social and Political Theory of P.-J. Proudhon* (Urbana: University of Illinois Press, 1972), 139–41.

15. Richard Vernon raises this issue in his introduction to Proudhon, *The Principle of Federation* (Toronto: University of Toronto Press, 1979).

16. Woodcock, *Proudhon*, 89.

17. See Joll, *The Anarchists,* for a conventional view of the activist Bakunin. Also Paul Avrich, *Anarchist Portraits* (Princeton: Princeton University Press, 1988). For a sharply dissenting and indeed demolishing view, see Aileen Kelly, *Mikhail Bakunin: A Study in the Psychology and Politics of Utopianism* (New York: Oxford University Press, 1982).

18. Bakunin, like Proudhon, nevertheless attacked Rousseau's notion of the social contract. See Paul Avrich's introduction in Bakunin, *God and the State* (New York: Dover, 1970), xi.

19. See Kelly, *Mikhail Bakunin*, 210ff.

20. Bakunin, *God and the State*, 24–26.

21. See Kelly, *Mikhail Bakunin*, 237–45.

22. This is the harshly critical reading of Aileen Kelly, who deflates the image of Bakunin as heroic revolutionary activist.

23. See "Bakunin and Nechaev" in Avrich, *Anarchist Portraits*, 38, 39.

24. After World War II, the Canadian anarchist historian George Woodcock encountered a group of Doukhobors in British Columbia. He knew of Kropotkin's description and was disappointed to find them more theocratic than libertarian. See Woodcock's autobiography, *Beyond the Blue Mountains* (Markham, Ontario: Fitzhenry and Whiteside, 1987), 1–13.

25. Jean Maitron, *Le Mouvement Anarchiste en France*, vol. I (Paris: Maspero, 1975), 152; Caroline Cahm, *Kropotkin and the Rise of Revolutionary Anarchism, 1872–1886* (Cambridge: Cambridge University Press, 1989), 182.

26. Cahm, *Kropotkin*, 12, 13.

27. Peter Kropotkin, "Mutual Aid," in Emile Capouya and Keitha Tompkins, eds., *The Essential Kropotkin* (New York: Liveright, 1975), 183.

28. Avrich, *Anarchist Portraits*, 72.

29. Quoted in Martin Buber, *Paths to Utopia*, trans. R. F. C. Hull (New York: Macmillan, 1950), 43.

30. This description of Kropotkin's last years has been taken largely from Avrich, *Anarchist Portraits*, 69, 70.

31. See Eugene Lunn, *Prophet of Community: The Romantic Socialism of Gustav Landauer* (Berkeley: University of California Press, 1973), 3.

32. Landauer, quoted in Avrich, *Anarchist Portraits*, 252.

33. Buber, *Paths to Utopia*, 53.

3. THE ANARCHIST MOVEMENT

1. Eugene Lunn, *Prophet of Community: The Romantic Socialism of Gustav Landauer* (Berkeley: University of California Press, 1973), 114–17.

2. James Joll, *The Anarchists* 2d ed. 186–88.

3. Kathryn Amdur, *Syndicalist Legacy: Trade Unions and Politics in Two French Cities in the Era of World War I* (Urbana: University of Illinois Press, 1986), 53; Barbara Mitchell, *The Practical Revolutionaries: A New Interpretation of the French Anarchosyndicalists* (Westport, Conn.: Greenwood, 1987), 39, 40.

4. Carolin Cahm, *Kropotkin and the Rise of Revolutionary Anarchism, 1872–1886* (Cambridge: Cambridge University Press, 1989), 76ff; Paul Avrich, *Anarchist Portraits* (Princeton: Princeton University Press, 1988), 243, 244.

5. See Ze'ev Iviansky, "Individual Terror: Concept and Typology," *Journal of Contemporary History* 12 (1977): 52.

6. See Richard Sonn, *Anarchism and Cultural Politics in Fin de Siècle France* (Lincoln: University of Nebraska Press, 1989), especially chaps. 3, 4, and 5, for a discussion of anarchist uses of popular culture.

7. For Picasso's involvement with anarchism, see Patricia Leighten, *Re-Ordering the Universe: Picasso and Anarchism, 1897–1914* (Princeton: Princeton University Press), 1989. Leighten is currently working on a broader study tentatively entitled *Anarchist Paradigms of the Parisian Avant-Garde, 1900–1914*, which will include Frantisek Kupka, Louis Marcoussis, and Juan Gris, among others. For a cautionary note concerning the distinction between anarchist flirtation and actual political involvement, see John Richardson, *A Life of Picasso, 1881–1906* Vol. I, (New York: Random House, 1991), 170–72.

8. Oscar Wilde, *The Soul of Man Under Socialism* (London: Humphreys, 1912), 54.

9. Francis Jourdain quoted in Sonn, *Anarchism and Cultural Politics,* 76.

10. See Murray Bookchin, *The Spanish Anarchists: The Heroic Years, 1868–1936* (New York: Free Life, 1977), 56, 59; and Joll, *The Anarchists,* 280.

11. Mitchell, *The Practical Revolutionaries,* 124ff.

12. Mitchell, *The Practical Revolutionaries,* 111ff; Joll, *The Anarchists,* 53; George Woodcock, *Pierre-Joseph Proudhon* (New York: Macmillan, 1956), 214, 215.

13. Kropotkin, "An Appeal to Artists," in Emile Capouya and Keitha Tompkins, eds., *The Essential Kropotkin,* (New York: Liveright, 1975), 23.

14. Peter Zarrow, *Anarchism and Chinese Political Culture* (New York: Columbia University Press, 1990), 150, 151.

15. See Margaret Marsh, *Anarchist Women, 1870–1920* (Philadelphia: Temple University Press, 1981), 46, 172, 181, and passim. Marsh focuses on American anarchist women; there has been little written on European anarchist-feminists.

16. Shirley Fredricks, "Feminism: The Essential Ingredient in Federica Montseny's Anarchist Theory," in Jane Slaughter and Robert Kern, eds., *European Women on the Left* (Westport, Conn.: Greenwood Press, 1981), 125–45.

17. Temma Kaplan, "Spanish Anarchism and Women's Liberation," *Journal of Contemporary History* 6, no.2 (1971): 109.

18. Mitchell, *The Practical Revolutionaries,* 87; Jean Maitron, *Le mouvement anarchiste en France,* vol. I, (Paris: Maspero, 1975), 344–48.

19. Maitron, *Le mouvement anarchiste en France,* vol. I, 349.

20. Maitron, *Le mouvement anarchiste en France,* vol. I, 357–60.

21. Joll, *The Anarchists,* 216.

22. Paul Avrich, *The Modern School Movement: Anarchism and Education in the U.S.* (Princeton: Princeton University Press, 1980), 26.

23. Avrich, *The Modern School Movement,* 32, 33.

24. Avrich, *The Modern School Movement,* 77–79.

25. Avrich, *The Modern School Movement,* 350, 351.

26. Mitchell, *The Practical Revolutionaries,* 233 ff; Joll, *The Anarchists,* 178, 179, 197, 198; Kathryn Amdur, *Syndicalist Legacy* (Urbana: University of Illinois, 1986), 267 ff; Carl Levy, "Italian Anarchism, 1870–1926," in David Goodway, ed., *For Anarchism* (London: Routledge, 1986), 56.

27. Maitron, *Le mouvement anarchiste en France,* vol. II, 52–55. Virtually all the information that follows on Russian anarchism has been taken from Paul Avrich, *The Russian Anarchists* (Princeton: Princeton University Press, 1967).

28. Avrich, *The Russian Anarchists*, 18, 19, 43.
29. Avrich, *The Russian Anarchists*, 161 ff.
30. Paul Avrich, *Anarchist Profiles*, 111–14.
31. Avrich, *Anarchist Profiles*, 118–21.

4. CASE STUDY: ANARCHISM IN SPAIN

1. For the hostility of Andalusian peasants to religion, see Jerome Mintz, *The Anarchists of Casas Viejas* (Chicago: University of Chicago Press, 1982), 20, 21, 63–77.
2. See Gerald Brenan, *The Spanish Labyrinth: An Account of the Social and Political Background of the Civil War* (Cambridge: Cambridge University Press, 1944), 42–55.
3. Eric Hobsbawn, *Primitive Rebels* (New York: Norton, 1959), 91.
4. See Temma Kaplan, *Anarchists of Andalusia, 1868–1903* (Princeton: Princeton University Press, 1977), 207–212; George Esenwein, *Anarchist Ideology and the Working-Class Movement in Spain, 1868–1898* (Berkeley: University of California Press, 1989), introduction; Jon Amsden, "Spanish Anarchism and the Stages Theory of History," *Radical History Review* 18, (1978): 66–75.
5. See Brenan, *The Spanish Labyrinth*, 130–40, and Esenwein, *Anarchist Ideology*, 14–21.
6. Esenwein, *Anarchist Ideology*, 63, 73.
7. Esenwein, *Anarchist Ideology*, 178–81.
8. Quoted in Esenwein, *Anarchist Ideology*, 186.
9. Jordi Getman, *Anarchism in Industrial Barcelona: Its Rural Roots* (unpublished honors thesis, University of Arkansas, 1991), 72.
10. Robert Kern, *Red Years/Black Years: A Political History of Spanish Anarchism, 1911–1937* (Philadelphia: ISHI, 1978), 81–104; Brenan, *The Spanish Labyrinth*, 255.
11. Mintz, *The Anarchists of Casas Viejas*, 180.
12. The information on Casas Viejas is taken from Mintz, *The Anarchists of Casas Viejas*, especially pp. 186–225.
13. *CNT*, 9 January 1933. Quoted in Mintz, *The Anarchists of Casas Viejas*, 267n.
14. Kern, *Red Years/Black Years*, 130–32.
15. Kern, *Red Years/Black Years*, 155–63. Kern cites a work by José Martín Blázquez (*I Helped Build an Army* [London: Secker and Warburg, 1939], 89–91) concerning the inefficiency of the militias, but tends to discount this criticism of these few formations.
16. Raymond Carr, *The Spanish Tragedy: The Civil War in Perspective* (London: Weidenfeld and Nicolson, 1977), 159.

17. George Orwell, *Homage to Catalonia* (Boston: Beacon Press, 1952), 4, 5.

18. Martha Ackelsberg, *Free Women of Spain: Anarchism and the Struggle for the Emancipation of Women* (Bloomington: Indiana University Press, 1991), 71, 72, 89, 118, 119, 128, and passim.

19. Hugh Thomas, "Agrarian Collectives in the Spanish Civil War," in Raymond Carr, ed., *The Republic and the Civil War in Spain* (London: Macmillan, 1971), 239–55.

20. Quoted in Burnett Bolloten, *The Spanish Revolution* (Chapel Hill: University of North Carolina Press, 1979), 71.

21. Bolloten, *The Spanish Revolution*, 73, 74. Most of the observers seem to have been foreign anarchists, like Augustin Souchy, who were inclined to idealize the anarchist collectives, so their reports must be taken with some scepticism. Certainly landless *braceros* would be more likely to accept the benefits of the collective than would former landowning peasants who were compelled to join in these circumstances. Even in these circumstances Souchy found freedom and tolerance; reporting that "collectivists and individualists live peacefully side by side" (p. 76).

22. Carr, *Spanish Tragedy*, 96–102; Kern, *Red Years/Black Years*, 170, 173; Burnett Bolloten, *The Grand Camouflage: The Spanish Civil War and Revolution, 1936–39* (London: Pall Mall Press, 1961), 48–52.

23. Carr, *Spanish Tragedy*, 108; Kern, *Red Years/Black Years*, 225–33.

24. Noam Chomsky, *American Power and the New Mandarins* (New York: Pantheon, 1967, 1969), 103, 104.

25. Robert Kern, "Anarchist Principles and Spanish Reality: Emma Goldman as a Participant in the Spanish Civil War, 1936–39," *Journal of Contemporary History* 11, 283 (1976):237–60.

5. CONTEMPORARY ANARCHISM

1. George Woodcock, *Letter to the Past* (Toronto: Fitzhenry and Whiteside, 1982), 313.

2. Herbert Read, "Existentialism, Marxism, and Anarchism," in *Anarchy and Order* (1954; reprint, Boston: Beacon Press, 1970), 146.

3. See Arthur Salmon, *Poets of the Apocalyse* (Boston: Twayne, 1983), 91–115, for the literary context of this neo-Romantic movement.

4. Radical Decentralist Project, Resolution No. 1, May 1969, quoted in Howard J. Ehrlich et al., eds., *Reinventing Anarchy: What Are Anarchists Thinking These Days?* (London: Routledge and Kegan Paul, 1979), 123.

5. Daniel Cohn-Bendit and Gabriel Cohn-Bendit, *Obsolete Communism*, trans. Arnold Pomerans, (New York: McGraw-Hill, 1968), 18.

6. "The Walls of 1968," in Eugen Weber, ed., *The Western Tradition* 3rd ed. (Lexington, Mass.: D. C. Heath, 1972), 1003–1006.

7. Cohn-Bendit and Cohn-Bendit, *Obsolete Communism*, 253–55.

8. "Gangs of armed males" quotation from *Siren, A Journal of Anarcho-Feminism*, originally published in 1971. Quoted in Ehrlich, *Reinventing Anarchy*, 251.

9. Murray Bookchin argues provocatively that Hebrew pastoralism is the root of this stern, patriarchal tradition. In the harsh desert environment, wealth was counted in animals and sons, and women were peripheral. The chronic insecurity of nomadic life led people to create more terrible gods and to erect an epistemology of rule based on the harsh expression of male will. Male dominance of and separation from nature led directly to the sovereignty of Yahweh. See Bookchin, *The Ecology of Freedom: The Emergence and Dissolution of Hierarchy* (Palo Alto: Cheshire Books, 1982), 103, 104.

10. Peggy Kornegger, "Anarchism: The Feminist Connection," in Ehrlich et al., eds., *Reinventing Anarchy*, 239, 240.

11. Quoted in John Clark, *The Anarchist Moment* (Montreal: Black Rose, 1984), 114.

12. John Clark, *The Anarchist Moment*, 225.

13. Bookchin, *Ecology of Freedom*, 307.

14. Bookchin, *Ecology of Freedom*, 26.

15. Edward Abbey, "Down the River with Henry Thoreau," in Abbey, ed., *The Best of Edward Abbey* (San Francisco: Sierra Club, 1984), 273.

16. Murray Bookchin, "Social Ecology vs. Deep Ecology," *Socialist Review* 18, no. 3 (July-September 1988): 19.

17. Greil Marcus, *Lipstick Traces: A Secret History of the Twentieth Century* (Cambridge, Mass.: Harvard University Press, 1989), 353–57.

18. Guy Debord, *Society of the Spectacle* (Detroit: Red and Black, 1977), paragraphs 23, 24.

19. Marcus, *Lipstick Traces*, 429.

20. Marcus, *Lipstick Traces*, 440–47.

21. See Richard Sonn, *Anarchism and Cultural Politics in Fin de Siècle France* (Lincoln: University of Nebraska Press, 1989), 270–72; Karl Mannheim, *Ideology and Utopia* (New York: Harcourt, Brace and World, 1961), 215, 225, 226.

22. See Martin Jay, "No Power to the Soviets," *Salmagundi* 88–89, (Fall 1990–Winter 1991).

23. There is another movement that conjoins anarchist distrust of the state with acceptance of the free market economy. This is the ideology of the Libertarian party, whose major spokesman in the United

States is the economist Murray Rothbard. While Rothbard's version of libertarianism bears some resemblance to anarchism, the party's total devotion to individual liberty, without anarchism's countervailing stress on community and hatred of exploitation, distances it from the anarchist tradition. Modern libertarians are much closer to the nineteenth-century classical liberals, who idealized laissez-faire capitalism operating within a minimal, "night-watchman" state. See Murray N. Rothbard, *Left and Right: The Prospects for Liberty* (Washington, D.C.: Cato Institute, 1979).

Bibliographic Essay

Primary Sources

There are a number of good anthologies in English of the writings of the nineteenth-century fathers of anarchism. These books include Robert L. Hoffman, ed. and trans., *Anarchism* (New York: Atherton, 1970); Irving L. Horowitz, ed., *The Anarchists* (New York: Dell, 1964), with an excellent introduction by the editor; Leonard Krimerman and Lewis Parry, eds., *Patterns of Anarchy* (New York: Doubleday, 1966); Marshall Shatz, ed., *The Essential Works of Anarchism* (New York: Quadrangle, 1972); and George Woodcock, ed., *The Anarchist Reader* (Sussex: Harvester, 1977).

Anthologies of the works of particular anarchist thinkers include Stewart Edwards, ed., *Selected Writings of Pierre-Joseph Proudhon* (New York: Doubleday, 1969); Emile Capouya and Keitha Tompkins, eds., *The Essential Kropotkin* (New York: Liveright, 1975); Martin Miller, ed., *P. A. Kropotkin: Selected Readings on Anarchism and Revolution*; (Cambridge, Mass.: MIT, 1970); Arthur Lehning, ed., *Michael Bakunin: Selected Writings* (New York: Grove, 1975); Robert Cutler, ed., *From Out of the Dustbin: Mikhail Bakunin's Basic Writings, 1869–1871* (Ann Arbor: Ardis, 1985).

A few of the key individual works by these thinkers are William Godwin's *Enquiry Concerning Political Justice*, edited by Isaac Kramnick (Harmondsworth, England: Penguin, 1976); Proudhon's *What Is Property?* (New York: Dover, 1970) and *The Principle of Federation*, edited by Richard Vernon (Toronto: University of Toronto Press, 1979); Stirner's *The Ego and His Own*, edited by John Carroll (New York: Harper & Row, 1971); and Bakunin's *God and the State* (New York: Dover, 1970).

Kropotkin wrote a number of books of great importance, including his autobiographical *Memoirs of a Revolutionist* (Boston: Houghton Mifflin, 1905); *The Conquest of Bread,* edited by Paul Avrich (Harmondsworth, England: Penguin, 1972); *Fields, Factories and Workshops,* edited by Colin Ward (New York: Harper & Row, 1975); and *Mutual Aid, a Factor in Evolution* (London: Heinemann, 1902). Kropotkin's article on anarchism in the 1910 *Encyclopedia Britannica* (11th ed.) furnishes an excellent brief overview.

Emma Goldman's three-volume autobiography, *Living My Life* (New York: Knopf, 1931) provides an American perspective on anarchism, along with her book *Anarchism and Other Essays* (New York: Mother Earth, 1910). Goldman's friend and fellow anarchist Alexander Berkman wrote the classic *Prison Memoirs of an Anarchist* (New York: Schocken, 1976). Goldman and Berkman's correspondence is published in Richard Drinnon and Anna Maria Drinnon, eds., *Nowhere at Home* (New York: Schocken, 1976).

A useful if rather slanted collection of eyewitness accounts of the Spanish civil war from an anarchist point of view is found in Sam Dolgoff, ed., *The Anarchist Collectives: Workers' Self-Management in Spain, 1936–1939* (Montreal: Black Rose, 1974). Daniel Cohn-Bendit, *Obsolete Communism* (New York: McGraw-Hill, 1968), is a good source on the events of May 1968 in France. Howard J. Ehrlich et al., eds., *Reinventing Anarchy: What Are Anarchists Thinking These Days?* (London: Routledge and Kegan Paul, 1979), is a useful compendium of anarchist thinking in the 1960s and 1970s. For the Situationist movement, see Guy Debord, *Society of the Spectacle* (Detroit: Red and Black, 1977).

Secondary Sources

The best general secondary works on the history of anarchism in English are James Joll, *The Anarchists,* 2d ed. (Cambridge: Harvard University Press, 1980), and George Woodcock, *Anarchism: A History of Libertarian Ideas and Movements* (New York: Meridian, 1962). A good collection of philosophical essays is in *Anarchism, Nomos XIX,* J. Roland Pennock and John Chapman, eds. (New York: New York University Press, 1978). Another excellent collection is David Goodway, ed., *For Anarchism: History, Theory and Practice* (London: Routledge, and Kegan Paul, 1986), which includes articles on anarchist movements outside Europe. Paul Avrich's *Anarchist Portraits* (Princeton: Princeton University Press, 1988) is a wide-ranging collection that focuses especially on Russian and American anarchists but also includes essays on the Paris Commune and Gustav Landauer. *Anarchism: From Theory to Practice,*

Daniel Guerin (New York: Monthly Review, 1970) is a brief book by an important French anarchist. Alan Ritter's *Anarchism: A Theoretical Analysis* (Cambridge: Cambridge University, 1980) takes a new look at the thought of anarchism's founding fathers.

Studies of individual anarchist thinkers include Isaac Krammick, *The Politics of Political Philosophy, a Case Study: Godwin's Anarchism and Radical England* (New Haven: Yale University Press, 1970); R. W. K. Paterson, *The Nihilistic Egoist: Max Stirner* (New York: Oxford University Press, 1971); John Carroll, *Break-Out from the Crystal Palace, the Anarcho-Psychological Critique: Stirner, Nietzsche, Dostoevsky* (London: Routledge and Kegan Paul, 1974); George Woodcock, *Pierre-Joseph Proudhon* (New York: Macmillan, 1956); Alan Ritter, *The Political Thought of Pierre-Joseph Proudhon* (Princeton: Princeton University Press, 1969); Robert L. Hoffman, *Revolutionary Justice: The Social and Political Theory of P.-J. Proudhon* (Urbana: University of Illinois Press, 1972). A brilliant and hostile portrayal of Bakunin is contained in Aileen Kelly, *Mikhail Bakunin: A Study in the Psychology and Politics of Utopianism* (New York: Oxford University Press, 1982). The standard biography is by E. H. Carr: *Michael Bakunin* (New York: Octagon, 1975). For Karl Marx's reactions to Stirner, Proudhon, and Bakunin, see the very useful book by Paul Thomas, *Karl Marx and the Anarchists* (London: Routledge and Kegan Paul, 1980). For a solid scholarly study of Kropotkin, see Martin Miller, *Kropotkin* (Chicago: University of Chicago Press, 1976); also Caroline Cahm, *Kropotkin and the Rise of Revolutionary Anarchism, 1872–1886* (Cambridge: Cambridge University Press, 1989), and George Woodcock and Ivan Avakumovic, *The Anarchist Prince: Peter Kropotkin* (New York: Schocken, 1971). The best work on Landauer is Eugene Lunn, *Prophet of Community: The Romantic Socialism of Gustav Landauer* (Berkeley: University of California Press, 1973); see also Charles Maurer, *Call to Revolution: The Mystical Anarchism of Gustav Landauer* (Detroit: Wayne State University Press, 1971). Martin Buber's *Paths to Utopia*, translated by R. F. C. Hull (New York: Macmillan, 1950), includes good material on his mentor, Landauer, as well as on other aspects of anarchist thought. On Elisée Reclus, see Marie Fleming, *The Anarchist Way to Socialism: Elisée Reclus and Nineteenth-Century European Anarchism* (London: Croom Helm, 1979). For Errico Malatesta, see P. Holgate, *Malatesta* (London: Freedom, 1956), and Vernon Richards, ed., *Errico Malatesta: His Life and Ideas* (London: Freedom, 1965).

There are several topical approaches one may take toward anarchism. On anarchist feminism, Margaret Marsh, *Anarchist Women, 1870–1920* (Philadelphia: Temple University Press, 1981), has a strictly American focus. Martha Ackelsberg, *Free Women of Spain: Anarchism and the*

Struggle for the Emancipation of Women, (Bloomington: Indiana University Press, 1991), focuses on the Spanish civil war. There is a useful essay on Federica Montseny in Jane Slaughter and Robert Kern, eds., *European Women on the Left* (Westport, Conn.: Greenwood, 1981). There is a plethora of studies of Emma Goldman, beginning with Richard Drinnon's *Rebel in Paradise* (Chicago: University of Chicago Press, 1961), and continuing with David Porter, ed., *Vision on Fire, Emma Goldman on the Spanish Revolution* (New Paltz, N.Y.: Commonground, 1983); Candace Falk, *Love, Anarchy, and Emma Goldman*, (New York: Holt, Rinehart and Winston, 1984), and Alice Wexler, *Emma Goldman: An Intimate Life* (New York: Pantheon, 1984). The Ehrlich anthology already mentioned, *Reinventing Anarchy*, has a section on current feminist thinking in the movement.

For the cultural ramifications of anarchism, see Richard Sonn, *Anarchism and Cultural Politics in Fin de Siècle France* (Lincoln: University of Nebraska Press, 1989); Joan Halperin, *Félix Fénéon, Aesthete and Anarchist in Fin de Siècle Paris* (New Haven: Yale, 1988); and Patricia Leighten, *Re-Ordering the Universe: Picasso and Anarchism, 1897–1914*, (Princeton: Princeton University Press, 1989). Herbert Read was perhaps the outstanding English anarchist intellectual. See his *Poetry and Anarchism* (New York: Macmillan, 1939) and *To Hell with Culture* (London: Routledge, 1941). A compilation of Read's essays can be found in *Anarchy and Order* (1954; reprint, Boston: Beacon Press, 1971). George Woodcock discussed the larger issue of *The Writer and Politics* (London: Porcupine, 1948). Salvatore Salerni, *Red November, Black November: Culture and Community in the IWW* (Albany, N.Y.: State University of New York, 1989), emphasizes the cultural bonds linking the American syndicalists.

Since the days of Francisco Ferrer, anarchists have viewed education as critical in reshaping people's attitudes. Paul Goodman, in *Growing Up Absurd* (New York: Random House 1960) and *Compulsory Miseducation* (Harmondsworth, England: Penguin, 1971), and A. S. Neill, in *Summerhill: A Radical Approach to Child Rearing* (New York: Hart, 1960), have continued the anarchist-educationalist tradition. On Neill, see Ray Hemmings, *Fifty Years of Freedom* (London: Allen and Unwin, 1972). On education in the United States, see Paul Avrich, *The Modern School Movement: Anarchism and Education in the U.S.* (Princeton: Princeton University Press, 1980), and Laurence Veysey, *The Communal Experience: Anarchist and Mystical Counter-Cultures in America* (New York: Harper & Row, 1973).

There are quite a few studies of anarcho-syndicalism, especially pertaining to France and to the syndicalist theorist Georges Sorel. A general study is *Anarcho-Syndicalism*, by the anarchist Rudolph Rocker

(London: Seeker and Warburg, 1938). See Sorel's seminal book, *Reflections on Violence* (London: Macmillan, 1961), and *The Illusions of Progress* (Berkeley: University of California Press, 1969). On Sorel's thought, see Irving Horowitz, *Radicalism and the Revolt Against Reason* (London: Routledge, 1961). For French syndicalism in theory and practice, see Barbara Mitchell, *The Practical Revolutionaries: A New Interpretation of the French Anarchosyndicalists* (Westport, Conn.: Greenwood, 1987); Kathryn Amdur, *Syndicalist Legacy* (Urbana: University of Illinois Press, 1986); F. F. Ridley, *Revolutionary Syndicalism in France* (Cambridge: Cambridge University Press, 1970); and Jeremy Jennings, *Syndicalism in France* (New York: St. Martin's, 1990). For Spanish syndicalism, the best studies in English are contained in broader works, such as Gerald Brenan's still-useful classic, *The Spanish Labyrinth*, 2d ed. (Cambridge: Cambridge University Press, 1950); Robert Kern's, *Red Years/Black Years: A Political History of Spanish Anarchism, 1911–1937* (Philadelphia: ISHI, 1978); and Murray Bookchin's *The Spanish Anarchists: The Heroic Years, 1868–1936* (New York: Free Life, 1977). In Spanish, see John Brademas, *Anarcosindicalismo y revolución en España (1930–1937)* (Barcelona: Ariel, 1974). On the American syndicalist organization, the IWW, see Melvyn Dubofsky, *We Shall Be All* (Urbana: University of Illinois Press, 1969); Steward Bird, Dan Georgakas, and Deborah Shaffer, *Solidarity Forever: An Oral History of the IWW* (Chicago: Lake View, 1985); and Dorothy Gallagher, *All the Right Enemies: The Life and Murder of Carlo Tresca* (New Brunswick, N.J.: Rutgers, 1988).

As the foregoing citations indicate, there are many histories of anarchism that focus on the experience of a particular nation. For the very important anarchist movement in Spain, one may also consult George Esenwein, *Anarchist Ideology and the Working-Class Movement in Spain, 1868–1898* (Berkeley: University of California Press, 1989); Temma Kaplan, *Anarchists of Andalusia, 1868–1903* (Princeton: Princeton University Press, 1977); and Jerome Mintz, *The Anarchists of Casas Viejas* (Chicago: University of Chicago Press, 1982), which is an unusual approach combining historical and anthropological perspectives. In this context, see also Eric Hobsbawm's seminal if much-disputed interpretation of Spanish anarchist millenarianism, *Primitive Rebels* (New York: Norton, 1959). Of the many literary evocations of the civil war, George Orwell's *Homage to Catalonia*, (Boston: Beacon Press, 1952) is indispensable for its portrayal of the anarchist-Stalinist conflict. Many other books on the Spanish civil war discuss the anarchist role in that conflict, such as Raymond Carr, *The Spanish Tragedy: The Civil War in Perspective* (London: Weidenfeld and Nicolson, 1977). An interesting partisan discussion of the Spanish civil war is included in Noam Chomsky,

American Power and the New Mandarins (New York: Pantheon, 1969). A specialized study from a partisan perspective is found in Juan Gomez Casas, *Anarchist Organization: The History of the F.A.I.* (Montreal: Black Rose, 1986).

The only overall study of French anarchism has not been translated into English; it is Jean Maitron's exhaustive two-volume *Le mouvement anarchiste en France* (Paris: Maspero, 1975). Reginald Carr, *Anarchism in France: The Case of Octave Mirbeau,* (Manchester, England: University of Manchester, 1977), deals with a literary anarchist of the 1890s, as do the cultural studies by Sonn and Halperin cited above. David Stafford, *From Anarchism to Reformism* (Toronto: University of Toronto, 1971), explores the political career of Dr. Paul Brousse. Andrew Carlson has dealt with the situation in Germany in *Anarchism in Germany* (Methuen, N.J.: Scarecrow, 1972); on Italian anarchism, see the chapter by Carl Levy in David Goodway, ed., *For Anarchism*, which also includes articles on Indian and Chinese anarchism. On China, see Peter Zarrow, *Anarchism and Chinese Political Culture* (New York: Columbia University Press, 1990); on India, see A. H. Doctor, *Anarchist Thought in India* (Bombay: Asia Publishing, 1964), and Geoffrey Ostergaard and Melville Correll, *The Gentle Anarchists* (Oxford: Clarendon, 1973). For anarchism in Russia, the works of Paul Avrich are essential: see *The Anarchists in the Russian Revolution* (Ithaca, N.Y.: Cornell University Press, 1973), *Kronstadt, 1921* (Princeton: Princeton University Press, 1970), and *The Russian Anarchists* (Princeton: Princeton University Press, 1967), as well as Part One of his book *Anarchist Portraits*. For English anarchism, see John Quail, *The Slow-Burning Fuse* (London: Granada, 1978), and Hermia Oliver, *The International Anarchist Movement in Late Victorian London* (London: Croom Helm, 1983). For anarchism in Mexico, see John Hart, *Anarchism and the Mexican Working Class, 1860–1931* (Austin: University of Texas Press, 1978). On Brazil, see John Dulles, *Anarchists and Communists in Brazil, 1900–1935* (Austin: University of Texas Press, 1973).

The collection of essays edited by David Apter and James Joll, *Anarchism Today* (Garden City, N.Y.: Doubleday, 1971), is a good place to begin to evaluate the sixties' impact on anarchism and vice versa. John Clark, *The Anarchist Moment* (Montreal: Black Rose, 1984), provides a good overview of the thought of Murray Bookchin. Bookchin's most important writings are *Post-Scarcity Anarchism* (Berkeley: Ramparts, 1971), *The Ecology of Freedom: The Emergence and Dissolution of Hierarchy* (Palo Alto: Cheshire, 1982), and *The Modern Crisis* (Philadelphia: New Society, 1986). Greil Marcus, *Lipstick Traces* (Cambridge, Mass.: Harvard University Press, 1989), provides an entertaining "secret history" that links dadaism, surrealism, punk rock, and the Situationists of Paris.

Anarchists have been evoked frequently in literature, by both admirers and detractors. Among the numerous novels featuring anarchists and dynamite in their plots are Henry James, *The Princess Casamassima* (New York: Macmillan, 1886); Joseph Conrad, *The Secret Agent* (Garden City: N.Y.: Doubleday, 1907); G. K. Chesterton, *The Man Who Was Thursday: A Nightmare* (1908; reprint, New York: Putnam, 1960); John Henry Mackay, *The Anarchists: A Picture of Civilization at the Close of the Nineteenth Century*; trans. George Schumm, (Boston: Benjamin Tucker, 1891); Émile Zola, *Paris* (Paris: Fasquelle, 1898); and Fyodor Dostoyevsky, *The Possessed* (New York: Macmillan, 1948). More recently, anarchist themes have surfaced in Ursula LeGuin, *The Dispossessed* (New York: Harper & Row, 1974); Bernard Malamud, *The Fixer* (New York: Farrar, Straus & Giraux, 1966); and in the novels of Edward Abbey, especially *The Monkey Wrench Gang* (New York: Avon, 1975). For a collection of Abbey's essays and excerpts from his novels, see Edward Abbey, ed., *The Best of Edward Abbey* (San Francisco: Sierra Club, 1984).

INDEX

The Author

Richard D. Sonn was born in Chicago, Illinois, where he attended public schools through high school. He received his bachelor's degree from the University of Michigan, Ann Arbor, and his master's and doctorate from the University of California, Berkeley. Since 1987 he has taught modern French history, social, cultural, and intellectual history, and historical method at the University of Arkansas, Fayetteville. He is the author of *Anarchism and Cultural Politics in Fin de Siècle France* (1989).

Professor Sonn lives on a farm outside of Prairie Grove, Arkansas, where he and his wife raise warmblood horses for dressage and jumping. They have two children, Julia and Alexander.

The Editor

Michael S. Roth is the Hartley Burr Alexander Professor of Humanities at Scripps College and professor of history at the Claremont Graduate School. He is the author of *Psycho-Analysis as History: Negation and Freedom in Freud* (1987) and *Knowing and History: Appropriations of Hegel in 20th-Century France* (1988), both published by Cornell University Press. He is currently writing about contemporary strategies for representing the past in the humanities and about conceptualizations of memory disorders in the nineteenth century.